G

Lorna Smith

# Carol Ann Duffy
# Simon Armitage
## & Pre-1914 Poetry

Series editor:
**Steve Eddy**

Philip Allan Updates
Market Place
Deddington
Oxfordshire
OX15 0SE

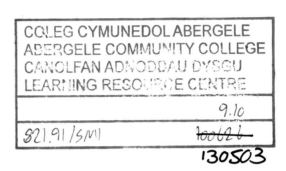
*Orders*

Bookpoint Ltd, 130 Milton Park, Abingdon, Oxfordshire, OX14 4SB
tel: 01235 827720
fax: 01235 400454
e-mail: uk.orders@bookpoint.co.uk
Lines are open 9.00 a.m.–5.00 p.m., Monday to Saturday, with a 24-hour message
answering service. You can also order through the Philip Allan Updates website:
www.philipallan.co.uk

© Philip Allan Updates 2005

ISBN 978-1-84489-228-0

Printed in Spain

Philip Allan Updates' policy is to use papers that are natural, renewable and
recyclable products and made from wood grown in sustainable forests. The
logging and manufacturing processes are expected to conform to the environ-
mental regulations of the country of origin.

P01042

# Contents

## Study and revision

## Context

## Poem by poem: Duffy

## Poem by poem: Armitage

# Poem by poem: Pre-1914 Poetry Bank

# Themes

# Style

# Comparing poems

# Tackling the exam

# Answers

# Glossary of literary terms .................................... 102

# Study and revision

This guide is intended for you to use throughout your GCSE English literature course. It will help you while you are studying the poems for the first time and later when you are revising. It explores in detail every poem in the AQA *Anthology* by Carol Ann Duffy and Simon Armitage, as well as all the poems in the Pre-1914 Poetry Bank. It makes suggestions for comparing poems and cross-referencing between them. Enjoy using it, and good luck in the exam!

## How to approach poetry

> Prose; words in their best order; — poetry; the *best* words in the best order.
>
> (Coleridge, *Table Talk*, 27 April 1823)

> Poetry is the record of the best and happiest moments of the happiest and best minds.
>
> (Shelley, *A Defence of Poetry*, 1821)

Perhaps the most important thing to remember about reading poetry is that it was written to be enjoyed and to inspire — not to be studied for an examination. Try to read each poem in the spirit in which it was intended to be read. It wasn't meant as a puzzle to be cracked or something to catch you out.

When you come to a poem for the first time, it is best to read it carefully all the way through. Don't stop at any unfamiliar words or ideas — reading the whole thing should give a sense of the feel and mood of the poem. This will help when you go back over any tricky areas. Then reread it several more times. Ask yourself what it is about and what thoughts and ideas the poet may have wanted you to come away with.

Ideally, read it *aloud* to yourself. That way, you will be reading it at the pace the poet intended. You may hear sound effects that you would not have noticed if you had only read it in your head.

# How to make the most of this guide

## Context

This section of the book gives background information on the two modern poets and some key themes. You will not be examined on this, but it is useful to understand something about the poets and their backgrounds when you read their work. The timeline also provides useful information on the pre-1914 poets.

## Poem by poem

Before reading the notes and information on any poem, it is important that you read the poem again to yourself — preferably several times. You may have read it already in class, but even so it's a good idea to refresh your memory before studying it.

### Key point

Top tip: One trick is to use removable sticky notes. Write down key points about a particular poem and stick the labels next to the poem in the *Anthology*. You can move the labels around easily, then remove the notes when you don't need them any more.

As you use this guide, it will be helpful to take notes — you will remember much more if you *write down* key facts. However, *remember that you are not allowed to use annotated poems in the examination.* You are allowed to annotate your class copy, but you will be given a clean copy before the exam.

* For each poem, first read through the 'Glossary' to check that you understand the less obvious words and phrases that it contains. Does this help you to understand a line that may have been puzzling you?

* The 'What happens?' paragraph is a brief summary of the 'story' of the poem and what it is about. It should give you an overview. There may be a 'Key point' box, which will give you extra information to help you understand the poem.

* The 'Structure', 'Language' and 'Imagery' sections should help you to explore the poem in more detail. Take your time over these. Look back at the poem to see each example in context and see if you can find *more* examples of the high-lighted features (such as rhyming couplets, alliteration or similes) so that you have plenty of evidence at your fingertips ready for the exam. These sections contain some key words in bold; many of them are explained in the 'Glossary of literary terms' at the end of the book.

* The 'Ideas to consider' section is one of the most important. It includes aspects that the poet wanted us to think carefully about — which is, perhaps, why they wrote the poem. You may simply be invited to share the poet's appreciation of a beautiful place, but often you will be drawn further. You might be encouraged to contemplate a new idea or to see something in a new light.

What point is the poet making? Is the poet successful in conveying his or her thoughts and attitudes? Where do your sympathies lie? Have your own thoughts and attitudes been influenced as a result? 'Pause for thought' boxes contain key questions. Read the questions carefully, considering the points they contain, and make your mind up. The answers will not be obvious and there is no clear right or wrong, so make sure that you can support your point of view using the text.

## Themes and style

When you have looked at all (or most of) the poems, read the sections of this book on 'Themes' and 'Style' carefully.

* 'Themes' looks at the poetry of Duffy and Armitage, identifying individual and shared themes. It gives you all you need to know about these modern poems in order to compare them to the pre-1914 texts.
* 'Style' contains information on viewpoint, setting and atmosphere, symbolism, imagery, rhythm, rhyme and metre, alliteration and assonance, and the poets' choice of language. It includes a table enabling you to compare the style of each modern poet with the pre-1914 poets.

## Comparing poems and tackling the exam

These final sections show you how to put everything together.

* 'Comparing poems' suggests how you can link poems by the same poet and by different poets. It includes a table of the main ways in which the poems might be compared and contrasted. It illustrates various ways in which you can plan essays, with some sample notes and paragraphs.
* 'Tackling the exam' gives hints on how to do as well as you can on the big day, with help on timing, planning your answer and choosing the right question for you. It includes handy opening phrases to use at various stages of your essay, along with some sample questions to practise with, and a sample A* answer.

# Weighing up the evidence

Having looked at what you should do, let's look at what you shouldn't do. There is no point in simply memorising chunks of this guide and regurgitating them in the examination, however secure this might make you feel.

Remember that the only way you are going to achieve good marks is to answer the question set on the exam paper. However well you have prepared, there is no way that you can predict exactly which poems the examiners will choose to focus on, and how the question about these poems will be worded. Your own thoughts and ideas will be recognised and valued by the examiners far more than prepared paragraphs. In other words, this guide should be seen as a

flexible tool for you to use to help shape and polish your own ideas — not a machine for turning out identical essays that don't quite do their job.

## Some useful websites

- **BBC Bitesize:** detailed notes on three representative poems by each of the four modern poets, plus five pre-1914 poems, with an interactive test on each one. www.bbc.co.uk/schools/gcsebitesize/english_literature
- **The Simon Armitage Website**: numerous links to various pages and sites, including a biography of Armitage, excerpts from his novels, examples of his poems and reviews. www.simonarmitage.co.uk
- **Contemporary Writers**: type 'Duffy' or 'Armitage' into the 'Search' box to access a biography and detailed list of their works. www.contemporarywriters.com
- **Andrew Moore's Teaching Resource Site**: brief yet comprehensive notes on all the poems in the anthology, plus all other GCSE texts. www.universalteacher.org.uk

# Context

As you read this section, ask yourself:
- ➤ What experiences from their own lives have Duffy and Armitage brought to their poems?
- ➤ How important is the background information in understanding the poems?
- ➤ What is interesting about the times in which the poets featured in the Pre-1914 Poetry Bank lived?

## Carol Ann Duffy

### Biography

Carol Ann Duffy was born in Glasgow in 1955. She grew up in Scotland and Staffordshire, attending local Catholic schools, before going to Liverpool University to study philosophy. After that she worked as a freelance writer in London and Manchester.

Carol Ann Duffy at the 1999 Whitbread Book Awards

She decided to be a poet when she was 14: 'for me [poetry has] always been a vocation, it's been a companion in my life and I think I actually would feel physically lonely if I didn't write poetry' (interview with Jane Bentham on the 'Young Writer' website: www.mystworld.com/youngwriter/authors/carolannduffy.html). She had her first work published when she was 16 years old. Her first main collection, *Fleshweathercock and Other Poems*, was published in 1974; she has since published over 20 other successful poetry titles and was able to take up full-time writing in 1985. She has won all the major awards for poetry and was presented with the OBE in 1995 and the CBE in 2001. Sean O'Brian, writing in *The Sunday Times*, referred to her as the representative poet of our time.

As well as writing poetry (including special collections for children), Carol Ann Duffy gives regular poetry readings. She also writes plays and radio plays, edits poetry and teaches creative writing. She now lives in Manchester with her partner (the poet Jackie Kay), her daughter, Ella — who was born in 1995 — and her dog.

## Background to the poems

Carol Ann Duffy's mother was Irish and, perhaps due to her influence, Duffy attended a Catholic primary school followed by a convent school. (In 'Before You Were Mine' Duffy describes walking home from Mass with her mother on Sunday mornings.) Christian references feature in several of the poems in the *Anthology*. Perhaps the nuns portrayed in 'Elvis's Twin Sister' were inspired by the Sisters Duffy met as a child. The more serious 'Salome' is based on a famous Bible story — Salome pleased Herod with her dancing and was rewarded with anything she chose; she asked for the head of John the Baptist. The character in 'Education for Leisure' talks of playing God, and spouts biblical language. However, when she was asked whether poetry is important in our secular society, Duffy said: 'It [is] for me: I don't believe in God' (article by Peter Forbes in *Guardian Review*, 31 August 2002).

## Feminism

Carol Ann Duffy is sometimes seen as a feminist poet. However, this does not necessarily mean that she champions women in her poetry at the expense of men — and she certainly does not in the selection in your *Anthology*. In 'Elvis's Twin Sister' and 'Anne Hathaway', she doesn't so much suggest that the women were behind great men as show them to be confident individuals, independent of Elvis and an equal of Shakespeare respectively. In 'Havisham' and 'Salome' we are given a distinctly unattractive view of women. The three final poems, 'We Remember Your Childhood Well', 'Education for Leisure' and 'Stealing' could be about a man or a woman. Perhaps it could be said that Duffy is a feminist because she features more women than men in her writing — but she does not set out to prove that women are superior.

**Pause for thought**

Carol Ann Duffy has said about writing: 'poetry can articulate ordinary people's feelings and worries and in some small way be a form of consolation or utterance for common humanity — very much in that way as a form of unholy prayer' (interview with Jane Bentham).

# Simon Armitage

## Biography

Simon Armitage was born in Huddersfield in 1963. He studied geography at Portsmouth Polytechnic and then worked with young offenders. This inspired him to study psychology and take a postgraduate qualification in social work at Manchester University. He then became a social worker.

According to one story, he was inspired to become a poet by an English teacher at school, who set the class the task of writing a poem about Christmas. The teacher promised that the six best poems would be put on the wall. Armitage says:

> I wrote about how my mum put sixpence in the Christmas pudding — which wasn't true — and he didn't put it on the wall. I thought he'd rumbled me, but he came up to me later and put his arm round me and said 'By the way, Simon, that was a really good poem', and I thought, 'Well, why didn't you put it on the f***ing wall, then?' And I've wondered since then if I've just been pursuing a revenge career. Every time I finish a piece I think, 'Put that on your wall!'

> (From a discussion with Robert Potts, *Guardian*, 15 December 1999.)

TopFoto

Armitage published his first volume of poetry, *Human Geography*, in 1986. He is a popular poet, often writes about subjects that appeal to the young, like football, and doesn't shy away from awkward subjects like drugs and drinking. As well as nine volumes of poetry, he has published two novels, stage plays, television and film screen-plays, has written work for the radio, and has edited collections of poetry. He was the official Millennium Poet, and chose to write about events that had been in the news during 1999, which made for grim reading.

He still lives in North Yorkshire, with his partner and their daughter Emily.

Simon Armitage

## Background to the poems

Armitage has had a variety of jobs in addition to writing and social work, including stacking supermarket shelves and DJ-ing. His writing makes him appear to be a very ordinary, everyday person — a typical 'guy next door'. The poems in the *Anthology* all feature events that might happen to any one of his readers — moving away from home ('Mother, any distance greater'), disagreeing with one's parents ('My father thought it bloody queer', 'Homecoming'), seeing others age and contemplating ageing oneself ('November', 'I've made out a will'). The two

most startling poems are not autobiographical but still deal with 'typical' topics: we have all heard of Batman and Robin, the subjects of 'Kid' — and perhaps Armitage was a childhood fan of the comic strip. 'Hitcher' is a dramatic tale, but one told about an average man in a boring job.

## Book of Matches

Some of the poems in the *Anthology* have been taken from Armitage's collection *Book of Matches*. (These are 'Mother, any distance greater', 'My father thought it bloody queer', 'Those bastards in their mansions' and 'I've made out a will'.) These are short untitled poems, supposed to be read aloud in the time it takes for a match to burn down — or 'before I'm bitten by the flame, and burnt' (from the first poem in the collection). There is obviously a pun in the title: 'book' relates to the volume of poetry itself as well as the little cardboard envelope that holds matches.

### Review your learning

Quick questions (answers are given on page 100):

**1** Which poet used to be a social worker?

**2** Which poet has lived in Glasgow, London and Manchester?

**3** Which poet is a CBE and OBE?

**4** Which poet was the official Millennium Poet?

Longer questions:

Do you agree with the following statements? Mark each one out of 5, where 5 means you strongly agree and 1 means you strongly disagree. Then write a short paragraph to explain your answers.

**5** A poet's background is a major influence on their work.

**6** It is not important for readers to know about a poet's background to understand the poems.

# Timeline

The timeline in Figure 1 shows Duffy and Armitage at the end of the range of British poets featured in your *Anthology*. As you can see, the majority of poems included in the *Anthology* were written during the nineteenth century, a particularly rich period of English literature. (However, don't assume that nothing of note was written between 1650 and 1750: it's just that the compilers of the *Anthology* did not happen to include anything.)

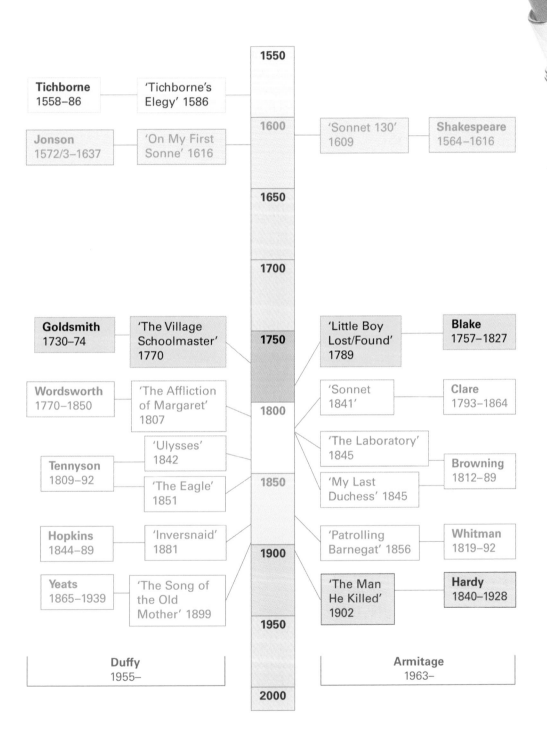

Figure 1 Timeline

# Poem by poem
# Duffy

## 'Havisham'

### What happens?

In the poem, Miss Havisham is seen to be still very bitter about her 'sweetheart bastard'. When she is alone, she wallows in her hatred and anger, wishing him dead and cursing him. Although she sometimes has passionate dreams of them lying together, when she wakes up she feels violent and even murderous towards him.

### Glossary

**slewed** (l. 8) pushed forcibly out of position
**puce** (l. 9) purple-brown

### Structure

The poem is composed of four quatrains. There is some **half-rhyme** (ll. 6 and 8, 'dress'/'this'), but this is very subtle, as there is **enjambement** which gives the impression of normal speech.

### Language

The poem is written in the **first person**, so we are presented with Miss Havisham's own thoughts. We do not know exactly who she is addressing. In the novel we only see her with other people, so it is interesting to see her here alone.

The violence in the poem shows the depth of Miss Havisham's hatred. She wishes her former lover 'dead' (l. 2). The mirror is 'slewed' (l. 8), presumably by Miss Havisham herself in a fit of rage, and she has 'stabbed' (l. 14) the cake.

**Pause for thought**

Look for other images of violence in the poem.

However, there is also love in the poem: the opening word is 'Beloved'. She has arousing dreams of him, decades on, 'my fluent tongue in [his] mouth' (l. 11).

The extent of Miss Havisham's love helps us to understand the betrayal she felt and the extent of her hatred. There is tension between the love and hate, shown through the **oxymoron** 'Beloved sweetheart bastard' (l. 1) and other contradictions in the poem like 'Love's/hate' (ll.12–13). Here the enjambement mirrors how Miss Havisham feels her life has been split apart.

We hear Miss Havisham's **tone** too, such as her desperation when she cries 'Nooooo' (l. 6) and her sobs when she claims 'it's [not] only the heart that b-b-b-breaks' (l. 16). This dramatic touch makes her more real for us.

The jumbled **syntax** illustrates her bitterness and confusion. For instance, the sentence, 'Spinster' (l. 5), seems spat out: she is disgusted by the fact she has never married. The muddled 'her, myself, who did this/to me?' (ll. 8–9) echoes her muddled thoughts.

Miss Havisham is clearly deranged. Duffy has given us details which reveal her fragile mental state: she does not wash ('I stink and remember', l. 5), spends days in bed, talks to her reflection in a mirror, even thinks about having 'a male corpse for a long, slow honeymoon' (l. 15).

## Imagery

Duffy uses **metaphor** to illustrate the bitterness felt by her protagonist. For example, the 'red balloon' of love bursts in her face when she is jilted (ll. 13–14); the image of the balloon illustrates how fragile and vulnerable love and happiness can be.

**Colour** is used in a dramatic way. Curses are 'Puce' (l. 9), a colour associated with dried blood or disease. 'Green' (l. 3) is linked to jealousy, 'yellowing' (l. 7) to autumn, 'white' (l. 13) with purity, and 'red' (l. 13) with love and passion.

The final line of the poem is like a challenge. We are given the image of a heart that breaks, but it is implied that other parts of the body 'break' as well. Perhaps Mis Havisham is thinking about her mind — her sense of reason has 'broken' too.

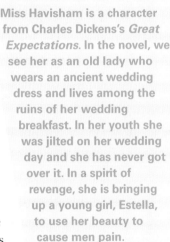

> **Key point**
>
> Miss Havisham is a character from Charles Dickens's *Great Expectations*. In the novel, we see her as an old lady who wears an ancient wedding dress and lives among the ruins of her wedding breakfast. In her youth she was jilted on her wedding day and she has never got over it. In a spirit of revenge, she is bringing up a young girl, Estella, to use her beauty to cause men pain.

## Ideas to consider

* Do you sympathise with Miss Havisham? Or is she simply wallowing in self-pity?
* When looking at her reflection, she asks 'who did this/to me?' (ll. 8–9). Who do you think is to blame for her desperate state?
* Throughout *Great Expectations*, she is referred to as Miss Havisham, but in the poem she is simply 'Havisham'. What is the effect of this?
* Is it the loss of her lover or her unmarried state — the fact that she is still a 'Spinster', in an age when the only career option for middle-class women was to marry — that affects her the most?

# 'Elvis's Twin Sister'

## What happens?

The poem is about Elvis Presley's fictional twin sister (Duffy made her up). She is a nun, living in a convent — a far cry from her brother's flamboyant rock-and-roll lifestyle. The poem makes the comparisons between their two lives humorous and cleverly includes references to some of Elvis's songs, yet there is a serious point to it. Elvis ended up living a solitary life, despite his money and fame, while his 'twin' is poor by choice but surrounded by affection and friends in her convent.

### Glossary

**immortal** *(l. 4)* living for ever, divine
**Gregorian chant** *(l. 11)* medieval-style religious chanting in unison by nuns and monks
**habit** *(l. 14)* a nun's dress
**wimple** *(l. 16)* cloth covering for a nun's head
**novice** *(l. 16)* a trainee nun
**Lawdy** *(l. 26)* slang for 'Praise the Lord', also used as an exclamation

## Structure

The poem is loosely in the form of a song. The short lines and irregular rhyme are reminiscent of the rock-and-roll style.

## Language

The poem is written in the **first person**, so we get a first-hand account of what it is like to be Elvis's twin. However, she is not given a name — we know her only as 'Sister Presley'.

There are some surprises, which add to the **humour** of the poem. For example, it is amusing that instead of praying for the souls of individuals, she prays for the 'immortal soul/of rock 'n' roll' (ll. 4–5). Similarly, we are surprised that Duffy uses the rock-and-roll slang term 'digs' (l. 9) to say that the Reverend Mother is impressed by Sister Presley's swinging walk, 'the way I move my hips' (l. 9), and by the fact that she wears 'blue suede shoes' (l. 20) under her habit.

**Key point**

The Latin *'Pascha nostrum immolatus est'* is the opening line of a Gregorian chant and means 'Our paschal lamb, Christ, has been sacrificed'. It is referring to Jesus' death on Good Friday.

There are many references to music. The first subtitle, 'Are you lonesome tonight? Do you miss me tonight?' is the main line from one of Elvis's songs. There is also the mention of 'blue suede shoes' — made famous by Elvis in a song recorded in 1956 — and the poem ends with lines from 'Heartbreak Hotel', another 1956 hit. These are balanced by details of one of the religious songs sung by Sister Presley in her convent (l. 13). Interestingly, this song is also about love, loss and pain — although of a different kind from that in Elvis's songs.

We are invited to make **comparisons** throughout between Elvis's superstar lifestyle and his sister's simple one. The contrasts don't always need spelling out. While Sister Presley 'tend[s] the gardens' (l. 2), we can imagine Elvis singing in front of a huge audience. While she wears 'a simple habit' (l. 14), Elvis's brash stage costumes are iconic.

## Imagery

There is effective word play in the fifth stanza. Sister Presley says that she thinks of her convent as 'Graceland' (l. 22), which is also the name of Elvis's mansion. In Christian terms, the state of grace is very important: being in a state of grace means to be inspired and to feel the strengthening influence of God. So the convent has been given God's blessing, which is why the nuns feel so comfortable there. Elvis was inspired to name his house Graceland by his own Christian beliefs, although it does not appear to have been such a happy home for him as his sister's home is for her.

Graceland was named for Elvis's Christian beliefs

## Ideas to consider

* While Elvis sings of 'Lonely Street' and 'Heartbreak Hotel' in the final stanza of the poem, his sister claims that she is 'alive and well' (l. 27). She seems happy and is surrounded by friends; Elvis died an undignified death, alone. Duffy is suggesting that it is better to be poor but among friends than rich and isolated.

**Pause for thought**

What is the poem suggesting about the values of today's society?

* Sister Presley seems to enjoy life — she swings her hips as she walks, she smiles her 'slow lopsided smile' (l. 24), and she lives in her own 'Graceland'. She is not restricted by too much formality either; she even uses slang — 'y'all' (l. 1) and the almost blasphemous 'Lawdy' (l. 26). Does she match the clichéd image of a straight-laced nun that many people hold?

# 'Anne Hathaway'

## What happens?

In the poem, Anne celebrates the gift of the bed, remembering the loving nights she and Shakespeare spent in it. The imagery recalls some of Shakespeare's plays and poems, and the lovers' bodies are likened to parts of speech combining to create a beautiful poem.

## Structure

The poem is in the form of a **sonnet**, which is highly appropriate given that Shakespeare wrote over 150 love sonnets. Although Shakespeare's sonnets kept to a strict rhyme scheme, this sonnet is freer — perhaps to express the freedom and lack of constraint that the couple experienced in their love making. However, the sonnet does end (as Shakespeare's did) with a **rhyming couplet**, emphasising Anne's firm intention to hold her husband's memory closely.

## Language

The poem is written in the **first person**, from the point of view of the newly widowed Anne. She remembers her husband with great love.

We are invited to **compare** the 'Romance/and drama' (ll. 9–10) played out in the Shakespeares' bed with the 'dribbling ... prose' (l. 12) that Anne assumes is taking place in the 'best' (l. 11) guest bed.

Anne remembers Shakespeare as her 'living laughing love' (l. 12). The light **alliteration** in these words helps to show that she is celebrating the life they had together rather than mourning his death.

## Imagery

Just like Shakespeare's works, the poem is full of **metaphor**. The first two lines list the romantic settings that the bed became for the lovers — 'a spinning world/of forests, castles, torchlight,

### Glossary

**assonance** *(l. 6)* a repeated vowel sound in a line of poetry, such as in John Clare's 'Sonnet', 'a wind sh<u>oo</u>k w<u>oo</u>d', and in Walt Whitman's 'Patrolling Barnegat', 'through h<u>oa</u>rse r<u>oa</u>r'

**prose** *(l. 12)* writing that is not poetry

**casket** *(l. 13)* a small ornamental box or chest in which to keep precious things like jewels, letters or cremated ashes

Shakespeare's house in Stratford-upon-Avon

clifftops, seas'. (All these settings appear in Shakespeare's plays. For example, the Forest of Arden is featured in *As You Like It*, castles appear in *Macbeth* and *Hamlet*, there are torchlit scenes in *Romeo and Juliet* and *A Midsummer Night's Dream*, *King Lear* includes a clifftop scene, and seas are important in *The Tempest* and *Twelfth Night*.) The variety of settings suggests the rich imagination that the couple shared — and perhaps the variety in their love making.

There is some wonderful **word play** in the poem. Duffy makes parts of speech, the tools Shakespeare used to create all his works, into metaphors of love. His 'words' become 'kisses' (ll. 3–4), their bodies 'rhyme' with 'echo' and 'assonance' (ll. 5–6), he is the 'verb' while she is the 'noun' (l. 7). The bed itself is the 'page' on which their 'drama' is written (ll. 8–10). While Anne and William make poetry, 'Romance' and drama together, their guests make 'prose'.

The language is **suggestive** and sexual: we can imagine what Shakespeare and Anne were doing as he 'dive[d] for pearls' (l. 3), when their bodies 'rhyme[d]' (l. 5) and when 'his touch' became 'a verb dancing in the centre' of her 'noun'.

The final rhyming couplet contains a **simile** as well as a metaphor: Anne holds her husband's memory in the 'casket' (l. 13) of her head as dearly as he held her in bed. A casket contains treasured contents: the memory of him is very precious to her. Significantly, a casket plays an important part in the love story of *The Merchant of Venice*.

## Key point

Anne Hathaway was 26 when she met the 18-year-old William Shakespeare. She became pregnant and they were married in 1582. Not a lot is known about Anne or the marriage. Some commentators have assumed that because Shakespeare only left his wife the 'second best bed' in his will the marriage was unhappy. However, as Duffy points out in the poem, the best bed would have been used for guests, and Shakespeare and his wife would have slept in the second best bed. Leaving it to her was a romantic gesture.

## Ideas to consider

* Does the rich imagery in the poem imply that Anne, too, had a talent for writing poetry? The sonnet suggests that making love with Anne inspired Shakespeare to create poetry; perhaps he also used ideas originally from *her* imagination in some of his greatest works.
* On the other hand, it could be suggested that Anne absorbed her husband's skill with words and so became able to write poetry herself.

## Pause for thought

Which opinion do you feel Duffy intends us to take: was Anne the inspiration for Shakespeare, or was she inspired by him?

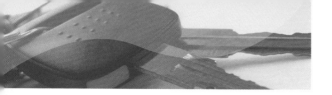

# 'Salome'

## What happens?

In the poem, Duffy creates a character who is used to casual sexual encounters with men and who is therefore not surprised to wake up and find a stranger's head on her pillow. However, she *is* surprised to find the head cold when she kisses it. She is hung over and resolves 'to clean up [her] act', so she flings back the covers to make the man get up. Only then does she see that the head on her pillow is not connected to the live body of a lover — she is shocked to find 'his head on a platter'. Carol Ann Duffy has altered history slightly to provide us with this comic yet tragic ending: there is nothing in the Bible about John the Baptist being killed in Salome's bed.

### Key point

Salome is a character who appears in the New Testament. She performed the 'dance of the seven veils' (probably a striptease) in front of Herod Antipas, the ruler of Palestine, who was so impressed that he offered to grant her any wish. She consulted with her mother and was prompted to ask for the head of John the Baptist on a platter. John was immediately executed.

## Structure

The poem is written in four stanzas of varying lengths. There is no rhyme pattern, but there is a repeated '-ter' rhyme running through the poem that becomes more intense towards its climax. (Look at 'latter', 'blighter', 'biter' and 'slaughter' in lines 28–31.) The use of this rhyme in the concluding punchline, 'his head on a platter', emphasises the horror of what has happened.

## Language

The poem is written in the **first person**, so we are given the opportunity to hear Salome speak for herself.

She immediately identifies herself as someone who is used to sleeping around: 'I'd done it before/(and doubtless I'll do it again' (ll. 1–2). She does not even seem embarrassed that she does not know who the man is: 'a head on the pillow beside me — whose? —/what did it matter?' (ll. 4–5). It takes four attempts for her to work out who it is: 'Peter?/Simon? Andrew? John?' (ll. 14–15). She is also proud of her conquests: the new man is 'Good-looking, of course' (l. 6), as if she wouldn't contemplate having a lover who was not good looking.

Duffy provides several clues that the man is dead. Salome states that the deep lines around his eyes are 'from pain, I'd guess' (l. 9), and his lips are 'Colder than pewter' (l. 13). It is **ironic** that while the poem's narrator cannot interpret these signs, we, the readers, know the story and so are aware of what has happened. There is literally just 'a head' (l. 4) on her pillow, with no body attached. It is

When the daughter of the said Herodias came in, and danced, and pleased Herod and them that sat with him, the king said unto the damsel, Ask of me whatsoever thou wilt, and I will give *it* thee.... And she went forth, and said unto her mother, What shall I ask? And she said, The head of John the Baptist.... And the king was exceeding sorry; *yet* for his oath's sake, and for their sakes which sat with him, he would not reject her. And immediately the king sent an executioner, and commanded his head to be brought: and he went and beheaded him in the prison, And brought his head in a charger, and gave it to the damsel: and the damsel gave it to her mother.

(Gospel according to Mark, ch. 6)

humorous that Salome has not worked this out, even though she recognises that something is strange.

Interestingly, Salome identifies her maid — who brings her tea and dry toast in an attempt to cure a hangover — as 'innocent' (l. 18). 'Innocent' is not an adjective that could be applied to Salome.

Salome uses a lot of **slang**. Rather than use the language of 2,000 years ago, Duffy gives Salome **modern idioms**. For example, she says she needs to 'cut out the booze and the fags and the sex' (l. 27) and calls the man beside her a 'blighter' (l. 29). The slang is particularly apparent in the final stanza when Salome pulls back the sheets and is shocked by what she sees — 'ain't life a bitch' (l. 35). There is more irony here, as she is talking about a *dead* person: life certainly had been a 'bitch' to John the Baptist.

## Imagery

Salome uses a **comparison** to express how cold the man's lips were when she kissed them — 'colder than pewter'. Unusually for the poem, this image fits the period in which the story is set.

There is an **ironic simile** in the third stanza. Salome comments that the man had come to her bed 'like a lamb to the slaughter' (l. 31). She meant that she was in control, the dominant one — she does not realise at this point that he really has been slaughtered.

**Pause for thought**

Do we learn more about Salome's character through what she tells us or through her style of speech?

## Ideas to consider

* When Salome says 'ain't life a bitch', do you think she is concerned for the dead man, or the repercussions that having a dead man in her bed will have for her?
* Do we sympathise with Salome in this predicament?
* Do you think the poem would make sense if we *didn't* know the story it is based on?

# 'Before You Were Mine'

## What happens?

The poet addresses this poem to her mother. She thinks of her mother's life before she, Duffy, was born — how she used to laugh with her friends, dance in a ballroom until late at night, walk home with a boyfriend. The poet also remembers her own childhood, when her mother taught her dance steps on the way home from Mass. Even then the poet yearned for her mother as she was once, sparkling and waltzing and laughing.

### Glossary

**Cha cha cha!** (*l. 16*) a ballroom dance with a Latin-American rhythm

**Portobello** (*l. 18*) a suburb of Edinburgh

## Structure

The poem is composed of four stanzas of five lines. Perhaps the regular pattern of the stanzas reminds us of the regularity of time passing.

## Language

The poem is written in the **first person**, but unlike 'Havisham', 'Salome', 'Elvis's Twin Sister' and 'Anne Hathaway', the narrator is not the main subject of the poem. Duffy does not take on a persona, as in the other poems, but writes as herself, 'remembering' her mother before she herself was born.

Duffy uses **natural, informal speech**: 'your Ma stands at the close/with a hiding for the late one' (ll. 9–10). She sounds as if she is chatting with her mother. At one point, though, she seems to take on the role of her mother's mother, chiding her daughter for having stayed out late with a boyfriend: 'and whose small bites on your neck, sweetheart?' (l. 15).

The poet thinks of her mother's life before she, Duffy, was born

The images of Duffy's mother are vividly described, even down to the way her mother and her two friends 'bend from the waist, holding/each other' (ll.3–4). The detail is almost photographic: perhaps the poet is looking at photos in an album. The reference to 'Marilyn' (l. 5) compares Duffy's mother with Marilyn Monroe in a famous photograph of the film star with her skirt blowing up.

It is interesting that the poem is mainly about the past (we see her mother before she became a mother, and as a mother of the young Duffy), but is mainly written in the **present tense**. Perhaps this is because the past is still very real. Again it suggests that the poet is looking through a photograph album, because the pictures *are* in the present, the images frozen in time.

The life that her mother led was full of glamour and light. There is the mirror ball in the ballroom ('the ballroom with a thousand eyes', l. 7) the thought of 'movie tomorrows' (l. 7), a 'tree,/with its lights' (ll. 14–15) where she kissed a boyfriend, a sense of 'sparkle' (l. 20) that the poet knew her mother once had. Yet there is some idea that the glamour also continues after Duffy is born: her mother taught her to dance, 'stamping stars' (l. 17) on the pavement. This is a reference to the way in which the hard-wearing metal tips on their shoes created sparks like stars, a reminder of the sparkly days of her mother's youth.

## Imagery

Duffy's mother's dancing shoes are seen as 'relics' (l. 12). This implies that not only are they unused, but they have almost a religious significance for her and are treasured possessions still.

Duffy says that she sees her mother's 'ghost' (l. 13). This does not necessarily imply that her mother is dead; but that her youth is. Duffy is imagining her mother as she once was, crossing George Square, and the picture in her mind is so strong that she can almost see her mother's shadowy figure.

There is a vivid image of Duffy imagining her mother: she sees her 'clear as scent' (l. 14). Duffy has deliberately mixed up the senses to show how a particular smell can trigger a vivid image.

## Ideas to consider

* The poem contains various layers of time. There is Duffy's mother's life ten years before Duffy was born, Duffy as a baby with her 'loud, possessive yell' (l. 11), Duffy as a child walking home from Mass, and Duffy as an adult writing the poem. Which period do you feel is the most vivid?
* What is Duffy's attitude towards her mother's past? Is she:
  * admiring of her past?
  * wistful that she was not a part of the best times in her mother's life?
  * aware of the irony that the best times were had before she was born?
  * jealous of her mother's friends?

Perhaps she experiences all these emotions.

**Pause for thought**

Do you think Duffy wishes that her own life were as glamorous and carefree as her mother's once was?

# 'We Remember Your Childhood Well'

## What happens?

The poem is one half of a conversation between a parent and a grown-up child. The parent could be a mother or a father, or perhaps both are present: it is not made explicit. (These notes assume that there is one parent — but see the first 'idea to consider' below.) Apparently the grown child is accusing the parent of harsh treatment they suffered when they were young — but we never hear the child's voice, only the parent's, who denies that anything bad ever happened.

## Structure

The poem consists of six three-line stanzas with an apparently random, loose **rhyme scheme** ('moors'/'door', ll. 2–3; 'fear'/'tears', ll. 14–15). The jerky rhythm is caused by short, staccato statements and echoes the prickly, hostile atmosphere.

## Language

The poem is written in the **first person**: Duffy has taken on the persona of one (or both) parents. It is significant that 'I' is never used — it is always 'we'. Whether or not both parents are present now, they certainly act as a team, a united front.

The poem is in the **past tense** because the parent is talking about what happened years ago. Crucially, however, the concluding stanza includes 'You *were* loved' (l. 17), which may suggest that the child is not loved any more.

Each stanza begins with a firm statement, usually a denial — 'Nobody hurt you' (l. 1) — except the last stanza, which opens with a question, 'What does it matter now?' (l. 16) There are further denials within the stanzas — the poem is full of **negatives**. ('Nobody' occurs five times.) The **repetition** emphasises the parent's refusal to admit that anything bad happened. The child is being ground down by repeated refutations.

We get an impression of the child through the parent's denials. Perhaps the child was over-imaginative: 'The bad man on the moors/was only a movie you saw' (ll. 2–3). Yet as the poem goes on, the parent becomes more menacing — 'we have the facts' (l. 10) — which suggests that the parents repressed the child, or worse. They

Publishing Pictures

The comic is personified so that the crackles of the fire become its laughter like to be in complete control and even change the subject when it suits them: 'You couldn't sing anyway, cared less' (l. 5).

It is interesting that the parent admits that some of the things the child mentions did happen, but insists that they happened in the way *they* remember it: 'You wanted to go that day. Begged' (l. 7). They seem to be trying to play a vicious mind game and change the way the child sees things.

The concluding stanza is painful. The parent denies they left 'skidmarks of sin/on your soul' (ll. 16–17), a frightening image. It seems the child has blamed the parents for ruining their life. In contrast, the final line contains only **positive**, affirming statements: 'We did what was best. We remember your childhood well.' Perhaps the parent is trying to undermine the child here and have the last word.

## Imagery

The action of the the second stanza is unclear: 'The moment's a blur, a *Film Fun*/laughing itself to death in the coal fire' (ll. 5–6). A comic is being burnt — the comic is **personified** so that the crackles of the fire become its laughter. Was the comic an escape route from an uncomfortable life? Did the parents throw the comic on the fire? Perhaps the burning comic symbolises the end of the child's 'fun'.

The parent sometimes uses **clichés** in order to belittle the child as much as possible — 'The whole thing is inside your head' (l. 9); 'We called the tune' (l. 10).

The idea of the 'secret police of your childhood' (l. 11) is disturbing. It suggests that the child was being stalked, their every moment monitored. Is the parent identifying with the 'police' or referring to other adults in the child's life, such as teachers? Certainly they had dominant voices: 'Boom. Boom. Boom' (l. 12).

## Ideas to consider

* We are unsure whether one or both parents are present: since there are no speech marks, it could be that we hear from one, then the other. Consider whether this makes a difference to our under-standing of the poem: one (elderly) parent against one (grown-up) child could suggest an even contest; two parents together against one child could appear very threatening.
* The parent, throughout, is seeking to justify their treatment of their child. Are they denying the truth to themselves as well as to the child?
* Despite the fact that the overwhelming sense in the poem is of sympathy for the child, we must remember that we, the reader, cannot be sure what happened in the past. Whose view do we trust — the child's or the parent's?

**Pause for thought**

Do you imagine the child to be a girl or a boy? Is there anything in the poem that suggests one or the other? We form our impression of the child entirely through the parent's words: is it important that we have a strong image of the child?

# 'Education for Leisure'

## What happens?

The poem is about a prospective murderer on the day leading up to their attack on a randomly chosen victim. The speaker has decided 'to kill something' simply to avoid being 'ignored' any more, and proceeds to kill a fly and a goldfish before going out armed with a bread-knife. Great tension is created at the end when we, the reader, become the prospective victim: 'I touch your arm.'

## Structure

The poem consists of five unrhymed quatrains. There is much **enjambement**, giving the lines the rhythm of natural speech.

## Language

The poem is written in the **first person**. Duffy has taken on a **persona**, yet we do not know anything about the speaker's appearance or home life or any personal details; we only learn what is revealed in the poem. We do not even know if the speaker is a man or a woman. ('He' is used in these notes, but remember 'he' could be a 'she'.)

The theme of death runs through the poem. The speaker announces 'I am going to kill something' in the opening sentence, which immediately creates tension — although we may not be too worried to begin with: 'something' is not the same as some*one*. He squashes a fly (l. 5) and 'pour[s] the goldfish down the bog' (l. 13), but apparently his killing spree is not yet over: the final stanza sees him going out with 'our bread-knife' (l. 19). The reader is left in suspense: we wonder whether he really *will* go on to murder us as he meets us in the street. The use of 'your' (l. 20) shocks us and involves us in the action.

The speaker uses **slang words**, such as 'bog' (l. 13), and **casual expressions**: 'I have had enough of being ignored' (l. 2), 'We did that at school' (l. 6). He did not learn much at school — he claims Shakespeare 'was in/another language' (ll. 6–7). However, he is obviously observant; he notices that 'The pavements glitter suddenly' (l. 20).

The speaker is deluded. He wants 'to play God' (l. 3) and sees himself as a 'genius' (l. 9) like Shakespeare. He claims to the radio DJ that he is a 'superstar' (l. 18).

The speaker has decided 'to kill something' and eventually goes out armed with a bread-knife

He clearly has a high opinion of himself: 'I', 'me' and 'my' appear 20 times. Yet we can see he is unemployed (he signs on every fortnight), with no obvious skills.

## Imagery

The reference to Shakespeare being 'in/another language' (ll. 6–7) is **ironic**. The speaker is referring to the difficulty he had in understanding the play at school, but we can see that Shakespeare *was* in another language for the prospective murderer, because the two plays suggested by line 5 (see Key point) plead for peace, not violence.

There is another literary allusion in the fourth stanza. Once he has flushed away the goldfish, he claims 'I see that it is good' (l. 14). This is an echo of the story in the Bible describing God's creation of the world, in which the end of each verse states: 'And God saw that it was good.' Again, the allusion is ironic: God created, the narrator destroys.

## Ideas to consider

* It is interesting to consider whether the impact of the poem would change if the narrator's gender was specified.
* Do you think the poem is supposed to be humorous? The speaker's casual attitude, his reference to the cat hiding because it 'knows I am a genius' (l. 12), the fate of the goldfish and the 'panicking' budgie (l. 14) could all come across as amusing. If we laugh at the poem, do you think that we are missing the point?
* The narrator seems to have lost his grip on reality: the poem contains more references to his imagined status than to his humdrum ordinary existence. He is more involved in his delusions of greatness than in the world in which he lives. Do you think it is possible to sympathise with him?
* Do you think he really does go on to commit a murder? What do you imagine happens immediately after the events described in the poem?

### Key point

The line 'I squash a fly against the window with my thumb' is a mixture of quotations from *King Lear* and *Romeo and Juliet*. Gloucester in *King Lear* (who has just been blinded) complains about how the gods seem to enjoy making people suffer: 'As flies to wanton boys are we to the gods/They kill us for their sport.' The two gangs in *Romeo and Juliet* accuse each other, 'Do you bite your thumb at us, sir?' — which was a rude gesture in Elizabethan times.

### Pause for thought

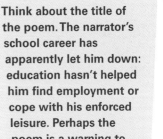

Think about the title of the poem. The narrator's school career has apparently let him down: education hasn't helped him find employment or cope with his enforced leisure. Perhaps the poem is a warning to our society — we need to ensure that people never get to such a state of emptiness that they have to delude themselves.

# 'Stealing'

## What happens?

The poem is half of a conversation between a self-confessed thief and an unidentified questioner. The thief is responding to the question 'What is the most unusual thing you ever stole?' He or she then describes stealing a snowman — and gives details about some other crimes too. We build up a picture of a disenchanted person who steals because they have nothing else to do and don't care about others.

## Structure

The poem consists of five equal stanzas of five lines each. There is much **enjambement**, allowing the lines to flow like natural speech. The rhythm is uneven: sentences are short and some words stand alone (like 'Again. Again', l. 18) to imitate the effect of someone speaking spontaneously. There is no end-rhyme but there is occasional **internal rhyme** to link ideas, such as 'slice'/'ice' (l. 4).

## Language

The poem is written in the **first person**. Duffy has taken on the **persona** of the thief. As in 'Education for Leisure', we know little about the speaker's background and do not even know if they are male or female. ('She' is used in these notes, but remember that 'she' could easily be 'he'.)

We gain an impression of the speaker through her words.

* She is strong because she carried the snowman even though 'He weighed a ton' (l. 7) — and is strong-minded too.
* She is obviously an accomplished thief, used to breaking into people's houses — and apparently has never been caught.
* She ignores people's feelings. She enjoys knowing that her actions provoke a response — 'Part of the thrill was knowing/that children would cry in the morning' (ll. 9–10) — and she enjoys leaving a mess.
* She is very selfish: 'Better off dead than giving in, not taking/what you want' (ll. 6–7). She is unconcerned about the effect her actions have on others.
* She acts out of boredom: 'Mostly I'm so bored I could eat myself' (l. 21). She does not need the things she steals — it just passes the time.
* Her casual attitude towards theft is suggested by her use of **colloquial language** and **slang** throughout — for example, 'mate' (l. 3), 'weighed a ton' (l. 7).

**Pause for thought**

To whom do you think the thief is speaking? It could be that she has been caught at last and is being interviewed by a policeman, or perhaps a social worker. On the other hand, it may be a casual acquaintance, someone she just felt like talking to.

* Perhaps the most disturbing aspect is the reason why she chose to steal the snowman: 'I wanted him, a mate/with a mind as cold as the slice of ice/within my own brain' (ll. 3–5). She is lonely and she feels her brain has iced over: there is no place for human warmth there now.

Many of the stolen items are associated with creativity, but the thief is unable to create things herself. She cannot play the guitar she stole (l. 22); she stole a bust of Shakespeare only to sell it on. Most bizarrely, she stole a snowman rather than make her own. Then she ruined it: 'I took a run/and booted him. Again. Again' (ll. 17–18). It seems she only knows how to destroy.

There is much **alliteration** in the poem. For example, the first stanza contains 'Midnight. He looked magnificent; a tall, white mute/beneath the winter moon.' The alliteration emphasises the association of ideas.

The **enjambement** suggests the pattern of natural speech but also has a dramatic role in the poem. 'I took a run/and booted him' (ll. 17–18) mimics how she planned a run up, paused, then kicked the snowman; the pause after 'might' in 'thought I might/learn to play' (ll. 22–3) hints that it was never a real intention.

## Imagery

The thief uses an effective **metaphor**, 'My breath ripped out/in rags' (ll. 18–19), to explain the physical effort of destroying the snowman. Rags are torn pieces of cloth; this image in a description of an act of destruction focuses on 'rags' that are themselves something destroyed.

The snowman could be a **symbol** for the speaker. It is significant that she sees the snowman as a 'mate' (l. 3), almost admitting she feels closer to the snowman than to any real person. The snowman is lonely; the speaker leads a solitary life and is apparently friendless. The snowman is cold; the speaker has a 'slice of ice' in her brain (l. 4) and stands 'alone amongst lumps of snow' (l. 20). The snowman is finally destroyed — will the speaker's actions ultimately be self-destructive?

## Ideas to consider

* Whoever she is speaking to, the thief is honest: she admits what she does and why she does it: 'Boredom' (l. 21). She is also confident enough to speak directly to her interviewer: 'You don't understand a word I'm saying, do you?' (l. 25). We understand what she is saying on a literal basis, but we cannot understand *why* she feels so alienated from society and acts as she does.
* Should we sympathise with the speaker? She may seem confident and boastful: 'Sometimes I steal things I don't need' (l. 11). However, she is also vulnerable, 'sick of the world' (l. 20). She is unable (or lacks the patience) to succeed or gain pleasure in the ways most of us do, such as by making our own snowman or learning to play the guitar.

# Poem by poem
# Armitage

## 'Mother, any distance greater'

### What happens?

Armitage has taken his mother to help him furnish his first home. As they take the measurements for new curtains, carpets and wallpaper, Armitage reflects on his relationship with his mother. She has always been there, an 'Anchor' (l. 8), and now Armitage is about to loose himself from her care. He admits he does not know what he will do without her: he may 'fall or fly' (l. 15).

### Glossary

**pelmet** *(l. 3)* a narrow cover hung over a window to conceal curtain rods

### Structure

The poem consists of two quatrains with lines of varying length, followed by a stanza of seven irregular lines. There is some **rhyme**, such as 'doors'/'floors' (ll. 3–4), and **half-rhyme**, 'span'/'hands' (ll. 1–2), but no regular rhyme pattern. Perhaps the most striking rhyme is the final couplet: 'sky'/'fly' (ll. 14–15).

### Language and imagery

The poem is written in the **second person**, directed to 'You', Armitage's mother.

The mother is seen as a necessary help in setting up her son's home. Armitage needs her not only because she provides 'a second pair of hands' (l. 2) but because she is experienced and she can use her traditional female homemaking skills.

The task seems daunting to Armitage. He uses **hyperbole** to describe 'the acres of the walls, the prairies of the floors' (l. 4). He has not bought a mansion — the rooms are probably quite small, but they feel enormous to Armitage because he has suddenly become aware of all the work he needs to do.

### Pause for thought

At 15 lines, the poem is *almost* a sonnet; the final four words just prevent it from being so. Sonnets are often associated with love. While this poem is undoubtedly about his love for his mother, perhaps Armitage wanted to suggest that he is leaving the safety of home by going beyond the 'safety' of the sonnet form.

The tape measure that they use becomes a **symbol** of the mother and son relationship. It is significant that she holds 'the zero-end' (l. 5): she was there at the 'zero' of Armitage's life, his birth. Reeling out the tape through the house symbolises 'unreeling/years between us' (ll. 7–8) as Armitage grew up. As he climbs — the tape getting longer and longer — he thinks of how he gradually became less dependent on her, but was still, crucially, connected to her. When he reaches 'the ladder to the loft' (l. 10) he realises he has reached breaking point — climbing any further would break the tape, as he is about to break a link with his mother by leaving the family home. His mother's 'fingertips still pinch/the last one-hundredth of an inch' (ll. 12–13). This suggests that life with her is safe and secure, and she doesn't want to let her son go. To consolidate the tape measure image, Armitage includes the **metaphor** of his mother as his 'Anchor' and him as a 'Kite' (l. 8). This suggests that she gives him security, but she limits his flight.

Armitage uses an amusing **image** of space-walking. He calls out the measurements 'back to base' (l. 6) — as if his mother were Ground Control — and 'space-walk[s]' (l. 9) through the bedrooms. He is walking through empty space because the rooms are not yet furnished, but the image is of him floating in space. This idea is extended when he reaches the 'hatch that opens on an endless sky' (l. 14) — and Armitage seems in real danger, as he does not know whether he will 'fall or fly' (l. 15).

The tape measure becomes a symbol of the mother and son relationship

Armitage uses **enjambement** to good effect: the pauses between lines echo the sense. For example, 'recording/length' (ll. 5–6) suggests the tugging to extend the measure, while we have to 'climb' from one line to another in 'climb/the ladder to the loft' (ll. 9–10).

## Ideas to consider

* There is a lot of love in the poem, under the prosaic surface of practical jobs associated with moving to a new home. The poet's love of his mother is clear from the first, tender word of the poem, 'Mother'. Her love of him is shown in the way she is helping him make his move even though she doesn't want to let him go.
* We assume that the poem is autobiographical, but this is not made obvious. It could be about anyone leaving the family home to set up on their own.
* Although the subject of the poem is Armitage leaving home, it could be read in the context of any fresh start or new life. It is about leaving the past behind and looking forward to the future, even though that future is unknown.

# 'My father thought it bloody queer'

## What happens?

This is the companion poem to 'Mother, any distance greater', and it reveals just as much love for the poet's father as the former poem did for his mother. The poem is about the day when Armitage came home with a pierced ear and dramatises his father's disdainful reaction. For some reason vivid memories of that day come flooding back to him years later.

## Structure

The poem consists of three stanzas of five, six and four lines. There is an irregular **rhyme scheme** — for example 'queer'/'ear', (ll. 1–2) and 'head'/'led'/'instead' (ll. 3–5) in the first stanza — which serves to provide echoes through the poem.

## Language

We assume the poem to be autobiographical. It is written in the **first person**.

The first two stanzas are written in the **past tense**. The final stanza is written in the **present tense** as, looking back, Armitage remembers his father's scornful response.

The poem is not written in strict chronological order. First it focuses on the father's reaction to the pierced ear — perhaps because that is what Armitage remembers most — *then* on the actual piercing of the ear.

We learn something about Armitage's father. He thought the earring was 'bloody queer' (l. 1); the words seem to be his, even though Armitage doesn't include quotation marks. 'Queer' can mean both 'strange' and 'homosexual' and the father may have disapproved of the earring on both counts. He rebukes his son, but does so with humour, likening his son to a prize bull that is led by a ring in its nose: 'If that's how easily you're led/you should've had it through your nose instead' (ll. 4–5). He seems to show affection for his son, despite his disappointment in him.

 **Pause for thought**

We wonder whether, now, the poet follows this advice and removes the earring as a sign of love for his father — or whether he retains the earring as a symbol of his own independence.

We also learn something about Armitage. He confesses that he wasn't brave enough to do the piercing himself, but used 'a jeweller's gun' (l. 8) and a friend's help 'to thread a sleeper in' (l. 10). Perhaps there is a sense of regret: he wanted to make a bold statement of his independence, but wasn't able to take the step in the way he thought he should.

The ending is **ambiguous** and unclear. For some reason, a long time later, Armitage is reminded of that day when he appeared with the earring. He is emotional — perhaps his father has died? His voice breaks 'like a tear' (l. 13) as he remembers from the depths of his consciousness, 'way back in the spiral of the ear' (l. 14), his father's sarcastic advice to 'take it out and leave it out next year' (l. 15). The words are more poignant and meaningful to him now.

## Imagery

Armitage enjoys **word play** in the second stanza, lightening the tone and contrasting with the sombre mood of the final stanza.

* He claims he 'hadn't had the <u>nerve</u> to numb/the lobe' (l .6), where 'nerve' can refer both to bravery and to the sensitive nerves under his skin that the needle would hurt.
* The sleeper (the silver ring that prevented the hole from healing over) 'slept' (l. 10), in a wry use of **personification**.
* This personification continues in the next line, which describes how the hole 'wept' (l. 11). This describes how the wound leaked pus, but also suggests the ear was 'weeping' for what had been done to it.

The image in the final stanza is complex and not easy to understand. Armitage uses **similes** to describe his voice 'breaking like a tear' and 'released like water' (l. 13). Perhaps he is referring to something that is unstoppable — you can't prevent tears from flowing, you can't stop rushing water. What have been released seem to be his father's words from the depths of his memory — 'the spiral of the ear' (l. 14) refers to the ear canal that goes deep into our heads. Since it is his 'own voice' (l. 13) that he hears, perhaps he is repeating to himself his father's words. It is interesting that 'tear' (l. 13) could also remind us that the ear has been *torn*. Again Armitage capitalises on word play.

## Ideas to consider

* The poem explores Armitage's independence. Presumably piercing his ear was an attempt to assert his independence and prove to himself — as well as his parents — that he was adult enough to be responsible for himself. However, the final stanza suggests that, even a long time later, Armitage is not fully independent of his father's influence.
* Armitage's love of his father comes through strongly even though it is not made explicit. The poet was obviously affected by his father's reaction, which is why he remembers his father's exact words so clearly. There is no hint in the poem that he thinks his father's views were wrong or that he resents these views; indeed, the final couplet seems to suggest that Armitage is realising that his father was right.

# 'Homecoming'

## What happens?

The poem invites us to hear about two vivid childhood memories — they are apparently unconnected, but we are asked to consider them 'both at once' (l. 1). The first is an 'exercise in trust' (l. 2) often used in drama lessons. The second is a family row caused because a favourite yellow jacket became dirtied at school. The poet uses the two memories to explore the nature of trust. Interestingly, they are not the speaker's memories, but the speaker's lover's; the memories are confided to the speaker 16 years later.

### Glossary

**makes a proper fist of it** *(l. 9)* slang: to make a poor attempt at something, do it badly

## Structure

The poem consists of four unequal stanzas of between four and seven lines. It is mostly written in **iambic pentameters**. Each stanza explores the idea of trust in a different way.

## Language

The poem is mainly written in the **second person**, to 'you'. However, 'you' is not addressed to the reader, but to one specific person. This person is anonymous; we learn little about him or her from the poem. (These notes assume that the subject is female, but this may not be the case.) The **first person** is not introduced until stanza 3 — 'I'm waiting by the phone' (l. 14). The poem could even be auto-biographical: perhaps it is Armitage himself waiting for his lover to ring.

The poem is written in the **present tense**, even though it is describing events that took place 16 years earlier. This adds immediacy and tension, making the events very real.

Armitage leaves it to the reader to fill the gaps that he has left in the narrative. We wonder exactly what happened to the yellow jacket — and exactly what caused the anger at home.

- The yellow jacket had somehow come off its peg and become 'scuffed and blackened underfoot' (l. 7). At home the mother, perhaps mistakenly, accuses her daughter of being careless and untrustworthy, 'makes a proper fist of it' (l. 9), and tempers are aroused on both sides. The daughter is sent to bed.
- The daughter is so incensed that she slips out at midnight to call someone from a phone-box — a friend? Perhaps the friend tells her she must 'Retrace' (l. 16) her steps home — the verb is an imperative, an order.
- When she returns someone is waiting for her: 'a father figure' (l. 17) — maybe not her father? — who 'wants to set things straight' (l. 17). It is not clear whether this means he wants to punish her or forgive her.

Perhaps a reconciliation with the 'father figure' never happened, because the episode is important enough for the girl to retell it to her lover 16 years later. As they embrace, the lover identifies parts of his body as features of the jacket — 'These ribs are pleats or seams...' (l. 18). As if repeating the trust exercise, he invites her to 'step backwards' (l. 21) and fall into his arms. Their bodies fit snugly together and it is as if the jacket 'still fits' (l. 23). It is only now that a true reconciliation with the past can take place. The lover has become the 'father figure' because he is able to comfort the girl and — crucially — show he trusts her.

Although the poem has a serious message, Armitage uses some wry phrases and **clichés**. For example, the mother is described in **hyperbole**, 'the very model of a model of a mother' (l. 8), a phrase which is intensified due to the **alliteration**. 'Questions/in the house' (ll. 10–11) describes the questions that were asked in the girl's home, but is a phrase usually relating to parliamentary questions in the House of Commons.

There is a vivid use of **colour** throughout the poem. The jacket is 'canary-yellow' (l. 5), but gets 'blackened' (l. 7); the angry daughter 'see[s] red' and someone screams 'Blue murder' (l. 11). The strong colours emphasise that the memory of the episode is still clear to the girl all those years later.

Armitage uses **enjambement** to great effect to echo the sense of some of the lines. When describing the trust exercise, he explains how someone will 'free-fall/backwards' (ll. 3–4) — the pause between the lines mimics the falling body.

### Pause for thought

We all fall out with our parents and friends for various reasons and it can be hard to trust others. Is there a message in the poem for us all?

## Imagery

The yellow jacket seems to have been a favourite garment and takes on a **symbolic** significance in the poem. Only when the imaginary jacket is found to 'still fit' in the final stanza can old wounds be healed.

## Ideas to consider

* A central **theme** in the poem is trust. The mother may have said that they could not trust the daughter to keep her coat clean: this small statement set off a chain of mistrust and hurt feelings.
* It is only when we have read the poem that the title becomes clear. There are three possible 'homecomings' in the poem: when the girl comes home with her dirty jacket, when she returns from the phone box at midnight, and when she finally feels trusted again in the final stanza. The girl can only psychologically return 'home' — a trusted place — after a reconciliation has taken place. 'Home' may now be in her lover's arms.

# 'November'

## What happens?

Armitage and a friend, John, are bringing John's grandmother to a hospital or care home to die. After they have settled her in, Armitage drives them both back to John's house where, depressed, they 'numb [them]selves with alcohol' (l. 12) and sit silently, contemplating their own approaching deaths. It is a melancholy poem — Armitage admits that 'the sun spangles', but only 'Sometimes' (l. 16).

## Structure

The poem consists of five stanzas of three lines and a final couplet. Perhaps this ending is a dark visual joke: we would have expected the last stanza to follow the pattern of the preceding ones and contain three lines, but this one has been cut off prematurely, or killed before its time.

The lines are long (containing 11 or 12 syllables) and so convey a sense of weight and heaviness, which suits the mood of the poem.

The poem dwells on the problems that old age brings

## Language and imagery

The poem is written in the **first person.** We assume that it is autobiographical, although it could be read with the speaker as a woman. (We will refer to Armitage himself as the narrator in these notes.)

The character of John is not fully introduced. We could assume that he is a friend (they drive back to *his* house), but the poem could conceivably be read with John as a relation or partner of the narrator.

There are a number of references to things drawing to a close:

* It is November, when the year is drawing to a close.
* The grandmother's life is drawing to a close: 'We have brought her here to die and we know it' (l. 3).
* They drive through 'the twilight zone' (l. 11) and sit at home at 'dusk' (l. 13), as the day is drawing to a close. They find the dusk terrifying: it reminds them of their own mortality. Just as they are powerless to prevent the grandmother's suffering (although they do all they can to make her comfortable), they are powerless to prevent the evening falling: 'we let it happen' (l. 15). By extension, it is also impossible for them to prevent their own ageing.

The poem dwells on the problems that old age brings. Armitage is brutally honest:

* The grandmother is weak: she takes 'four short steps to our two' (l. 2). She is treated like an object, dependent on others, when they 'parcel her' (l. 5) into her bed. She is incontinent.
* The other old women seem half-dead already, with their 'pasty bloodless smiles' (l. 7) and 'stunned brains' (l. 8). They are physically ugly, bald and with 'slack breasts' (l. 8).
* Armitage refers to the old women as 'monsters', but the horror for him lies in the fact that he and John are themselves 'almost these monsters' (l. 9). Soon they will both be old, weak and dependent too.

The ending of the poem offers little hope. The sun only sometimes 'spangles', enabling them to 'feel alive' (l. 16); even then there is a suggestion that they are obliged to do so and little indication that life can be pleasurable. Perhaps Armitage is encouraging us to wonder what life is for — what its 'meaning' is.

> **Key point**
>
> *The Twilight Zone* was an American science-fiction television series shown in the 1960s. It focused on life, death and life after death and was seen as new and perturbing. Armitage exploits the phrase 'the twilight zone', aware that the word play will make us think of the disturbing storylines as well as the time of day.

## Ideas to consider

* At one point Armitage speaks to John, although he has not signalled the speech with quotation marks or punctuation: 'It is time John' (l. 7). On one level he could mean that it is time for them to leave the grandmother (perhaps for the last time?) and that it is her time to die. On another level, maybe Armitage is referring to the lack of time he and John have left in their own lives. Armitage also addresses John in line 9, but it is not clear whether these words are his thoughts or his speech.
* The poem appears cold and shocking at times. Armitage describes how the grandmother 'sinks down into her incontinence' (l. 6), when we would have expected her to sink into a comfortable bed. The description of the old women as 'monsters' is also very chilling. Armitage is deliberately emphasising the difficulties that old age causes both to the elderly themselves and to their loved ones.
* There is no suggestion that either the grandmother or John and Armitage have any religious faith; for them, there is no comfort in the idea of an afterlife or rebirth of any sort. Do you think that the poem would be different if they did have such a faith?

# 'Kid'

## What happens?

The poem is told by Robin, now no longer with Batman: he is grown up and independent — and proud of being so. He's not afraid to put the record straight and has 'blown [Batman's] cover' (l. 7) by claiming that Batman was not the father figure to Robin that everyone assumed him to be. He tells a scandalous story of how Batman had an affair with a married woman — effectively ruining Batman's reputation. He enjoys painting a picture of Batman struggling over the preparation of a simple meal, now that he, Robin, is no longer around to cook it, and claims that only 'now', assertive and self-reliant, is he truly a 'boy wonder' (l. 24).

### Glossary

**leeward** *(l. 3)* towards the sheltered side

**scotched** *(l. 6)* put a stop to

## Structure

The poem consists of a series of 24 **trochaic pentameters**, all sharing the '-er' rhyme. (The one exception is 'motor' (l. 11), but the rhyme sounds the same.)

## Language

The poem is written in the **first person**. Armitage has imagined how Robin might have been and how he might have felt.

One of the most notable features of the poem is the **rhyme scheme**. It mimics the famous theme tune to the Batman television series, often chanted by children in the playground: -er -er -er -er, -er -er -er -er, Batman!'

The poem includes the use of **American slang**, such as 'the wild blue yonder' (l. 3) and 'let the cat out' (l. 9). The use of slang is effective, because as well as anchoring the poem firmly in the USA, it emphasises Robin's relaxed and casual attitude — especially when he uses slang that is disparaging towards Batman.

The poem is full of implicit and explicit **contrasts**. We imagine Batman and Robin as they once were, when Batman the 'big shot' (l. 1) gave orders to Robin; we then imagine them as they are now, with Batman discredited, hungry and bored, 'punching the palm of your hand' (l. 23), and Robin in a position of authority. The language used includes contrasts too — Robin claims that Batman 'let me loose to wander/...or ditched me, rather' (ll. 2–4), and he emphasises the

### Key point

This poem relies on us recognising the famous partnership of Batman and Robin, the Boy Wonder, who have starred together in comics, cartoons and films since the 1940s. Based in Gotham City (a fictional city in America), they save the world from various evil characters.

contrast in his clothes — he now wears 'a pair of jeans and crew-neck jumper' rather than his 'green and scarlet number' (ll. 16–17). Each of the contrasts shows the reversal in fortunes of Batman and Robin.

Robin's attitude towards Batman is clear. He mocks the newspaper headlines that carried his revelations of Batman's affair, 'Holy robin-redbreast-nest-egg-shocker!' (l. 12). He is scornful: 'I'm not playing ball boy any longer' (l. 14) (as if saving the world was as inconsequential as a game of tennis) and is glad that Batman is now in a weak position. He seems vindictive, particularly in the final line: 'you baby'. He, Robin, is 'baby' no longer, and it is Batman who is in need of care.

Typically, the poem contains **word play**. For example, 'caper' (l. 9) is a **pun**. Literally 'caper' refers to Batman's light-hearted affair, but it is also a reminder of the capes worn by Batman and Robin. Robin mocks his 'uniform' by using language more suited to the world of fashion ('green and scarlet number', l. 16).

The poem is **humorous** but it has a serious point to it. Robin is no longer blindly following a hero-figure, but is in charge of his own destiny.

Adam West and Burt Ward star as Batman and Robin in the popular American television series

## Imagery

Robin presents a **metaphor** of himself as Batman's 'shadow' (l. 20). Perhaps we should infer that, in serving Batman, Robin was also a 'shadow' of himself. Only when he is independent is he able fully to shine.

## Ideas to consider

* It is interesting to speculate how and why Batman parted company with Robin. Did he really 'ditch' him 'in the gutter' (ll. 4–5) as Robin suggests? Or was he being genuinely kind, letting him 'loose to wander' — perhaps because he realised that Robin needed to 'grow up' (l. 2) and be independent? Robin angrily assumes the former, but we only have his side of the story, so it's impossible to know for sure.
* Do you think the poem is relevant to us? Perhaps Armitage is warning us that idolising one particular hero is dangerous.
* Batman appears to be unable to function without Robin. Maybe this suggests that superheroes are not so 'super' after all.
* Why did Armitage choose to call the poem 'Kid'?

# 'Those bastards in their mansions'

## What happens?

This poem is a puzzle; Armitage gives little away. It is about the struggle of the poor against the rich. Most of the poem is hypothetical: the narrator, a poor man (a criminal?) tells us not what he *has* done, but what he *might* have done to cause the rich to 'shriek' (l. 2). The worst thing he could have done was to steal from the rich the 'gift of fire' (l. 6) to give it to the poor. All that is definite is that he carries a gun.

### Glossary

**cuffs** (l. 8) here, iron handcuffs

**shackles** (l. 8) metal loops used as restraints, placed around the ankle

## Structure

The poem is in the form of a **sonnet**. This is unusual: we associate sonnets with love (or grief) rather than protest poetry. Many of the lines **rhyme** (such as 'ditches'/'britches', ll. 3–4), but there is no regular scheme.

## Language

The poem is written in the **first person,** but we assume that it is not Armitage's own voice: he is using a **persona**.

It is not clear whether Armitage want us to imagine real 'mansions' (l. 1), 'palaces and castles' (l. 10), or whether he is exaggerating. He is clearly setting the wealthy upper classes up in **contrast** to the poor lower classes.

It is also not clear when the poem is set. It is written in the **present tense** to add to the sense of drama, but it includes **archaic** phrases such as 'stocking feet and threadbare britches' (l. 4) and 'cuffs and shackles' (l. 8). Armitage may want us to imagine a historical setting.

The speaker appears to be a kind of Robin Hood character, capable of robbing the rich of their fire to give to the poor. There is no love lost between the speaker and the rich: he calls them 'bastards' (l. 1). But it is important to remember that he never actually steals the fire — he just talks about doing so. We know that he prefers to 'stick to the shadows, carry a gun' (l. 14). Is the gun to protect himself or others?

### Pause for thought

The poem could be about Armitage's own poetry. The literary Robin Hood, writing for the poor (ordinary people), battles against 'bastards' who criticise his work. There are perhaps references to famous poets — Shakespeare (because it is a sonnet), Byron (because he wrote a great poem called 'Prometheus Unbound') and Tennyson ('The Eagle'). Byron and Tennyson were both Lords. Do they see Armitage as an enemy? Is Armitage making a point about his poetry challenging the literary establishment?

We never find out what makes the rich people 'shriek' in the first line. We know that they are anxious: their properties are guarded by 'dogs' and 'ditches' (l. 3), and even by 'eagles' (l. 12); their doors are locked and the poor are subjugated; the rich have the power to have someone 'pinned down, grilled beneath the sun' (l. 13).

**Key point**

*The story of the gift of fire*

According to Greek myth, Prometheus was the creator of mankind. The goddess Athene taught him great skills such as mathematics and medicine; he then taught them to humans. Zeus (father and ruler of the gods) became angry with Prometheus because, thanks to these skills, man was becoming too powerful.

When, later, Prometheus tricked Zeus, in revenge Zeus decreed that man should be prevented from using fire. Prometheus, however, secretly lit a torch from the sun and passed the gift of fire on to mankind.

As punishment, Zeus had Prometheus chained naked to a pillar in the mountains. A vulture tore at Prometheus' liver all day long, yet during the bitter cold of the mountain night, the liver became whole again. He was not freed for many years.

## Imagery

In both the myth and the poem, fire is a symbol of power. In Armitage's version, fire is the property of the rich. Yet it could have been used by the poor to melt the 'iron' (l. 9) from their 'cuffs and shackles' and turn them into weapons with which to attack the rich. The 'cuffs and shackles' may relate to physical restraints used on the poor (they remind us of those used by slave owners on their slaves), although the phrase is more probably a **metaphor** to suggest the social and economic restraints under which the poor lived (and still live).

## Ideas to consider

* The poem seems quite humorous. Do you think that it is making a serious point too? Is it a political poem?
* Does the suggestion that the narrator is prepared to use his gun imply that he is as bad as the rich?

**Pause for thought**

With whom do you sympathise as you read the poem — the rich who are targeted and robbed, or the poor? Is it possible to sympathise with both?

# 'I've made out a will'

## What happens?

In this simple, amusing poem, Armitage announces that he has made a will. It is not a will concerning what will happen to his goods and property after his death, but what will happen to his body. He is leaving it all to the National Health Service (NHS), presumably for research or transplant. The only part of his body that he does not want to donate is his heart.

### Glossary

**sprockets** (l. 10) cogwheels found in engines

## Structure

The poem is written in the form of a **sonnet**. We usually associate sonnets with love — perhaps this connects to Armitage's refusal to be separated from his heart.

There is some **rhyme** at the ends of lines (e.g. 'use'/'glues', ll. 2–3, 'bone'/ 'alone', ll. 7–8) as well as **internal rhymes** within some lines (e.g. 'myself'/'Health', ll. 1–2). The rhyme gives the poem a tight and controlled feel.

## Language and imagery

The poem is written in the **first person**. It may be partly autobiographical, although the poem is so exaggerated that it is unlikely that the will it describes is real.

Armitage refers to the parts of his body in humorous **metaphors**. The images are disparaging: he is making out that the elements he describes are not important. For example:

### Pause for thought ⏸

Which image do you think best fits how Armitage sees his body? Which image best fits how you see your body?

* The various arteries, veins, glands and fluids are seen as 'jellies and tubes and syrups and glues' (l. 3), which reduces these vital vessels and liquids to little more than ingredients for a children's party.
* The brains are 'a loaf' (l. 4), reminding us both of the spongy appearance of the brain and of the Cockney rhyming slang phrase 'use your loaf'. ('Head' rhymes with 'loaf of bread', shortened to 'loaf'.)
* His blood is 'bilberry soup' (l. 6), reminding us of blood's colour and consistency.

There are three **images** to describe his skeleton in line 7:

* a 'chassis', which refers to a car, perhaps with associations of speed and power
* a 'cage', which has connotations of safety but also of imprisonment
* a 'cathedral', which both reminds us of the tall, skeletal architecture of medieval cathedrals and suggests that there is something sacred about his body

The humour of the poem is emphasised through **alliteration**, such as 'blood' and 'bilberry', 'cage' and 'cathedral'.

Much of the poem is in the form of a list, with items linked by the simple connecting word 'and'. This gives the impression that Armitage could go on enumerating his body parts endlessly. He emphasises that his body is not perfect: he details the 'fillings and stitches and wounds' (l. 5) along with the vessels, fluids, bones and organs.

The last six lines of the sonnet (the sextet) contains an extended **metaphor** in which Armitage compares his body to a clock. This is a clever play on words, because both a clock and a body have a 'face' and 'hands' (l. 12), and the slang word 'ticker' (l. 13) is often used for the heart. A traditional clock is a precise piece of engineering — just like a body.

In the last six lines of the sonnet, Armitage compares his body to a clock

## Ideas to consider

* Armitage is emphatic that he does not want his heart to go to the NHS — he states this in lines 8 and 13–14 — but he does not explain *why*. (This is interesting, as the heart is one of the most valuable organs from a donation point of view.) We are left to guess.

* What do you think will happen to his heart, once the rest of his body has been passed to the NHS? He claims it should be left 'where it stops or hangs' (l. 14), which would be difficult if the rest of his body was going to be dismembered. Perhaps he wishes it to be buried or cremated. Or perhaps he has something else in mind?

* The poem raises questions about how far we can control things after our death.

* What is the poet's attitude to death? Armitage was still relatively young when he wrote the poem and unlikely to die for many years. Do you think his attitude would have been the same had he been writing as an old man?

**Pause for thought**

Do you think that he wants to retain his heart because it is associated with love? Maybe his love is too personal to be used for research or for transplant. Are there any other reasons why he may wish to retain his heart?

# 'Hitcher'

## What happens?

The poem tells a frightening story of a man who, disaffected with his work and feeling bored, decides on the spur of the moment to do something different. He drives around aimlessly, picks up a hitchhiker in Leeds and then, apparently unprovoked, attacks the man with a steering wheel lock and pushes him out of the moving car. We do not learn what happens to the hitcher (is he dead?), or what happens to the narrator, but it is clear that the narrator has no regrets about his actions.

## Structure

The poem consists of five regular stanzas of five lines each. In each one, the first line is short (4–6 syllables), the next line a little longer (7–11 syllables) and the next longer still (10–14). The fourth is then shorter again and the fifth shorter still. This makes each stanza resemble an arrow on the page.

### Pause for thought

Perhaps the differing line lengths dramatise the feelings that the driver experiences of moving swiftly from being calm and controlled to being exhilarated and out of control and then calm again.

## Language

The poem is written in the **first person** — but we can safely assume that Armitage has taken on a **persona** and is not writing from personal experience.

The poem is written in the **past tense** as the narrator recounts his memories. The narrator seems to be talking to someone, although there are no clues as to whom. Perhaps it is a policeman or a psychiatrist, or perhaps a friend; we are left to speculate.

The poem starts with what seems to be an excuse for the behaviour that follows ('I'd been tired, under/the weather', ll. 1–2) and the knowledge that he was about to lose his job ('*One more sick-note, mister, and you're finished. Fired*', l. 3). However, there is nothing further in the poem to explain why he did what he did, and he shows no remorse. This gives us the impression that his malingering was due to laziness rather than a genuine illness, and thus that there is no excuse at all for his violence.

The narrator includes precise information. For instance, he tells us the make of car, 'A Vauxhall Astra' (l. 5), the names of the towns he passed through and the fact that he hit the hitcher 'six times' (l. 13). This precision seems to contrast with the vague attitude of the hitchhiker, who claimed 'the truth/… was blowin' in the wind' (ll. 8–9) and that 'he liked the breeze/to run its fingers/through his hair' (ll. 20–22).

The hitchhiker is in some ways similar to the narrator — 'We were the same age, give or take a week' (l. 19); yet the differences between them are more marked. The hitcher is a relaxed hippie with few possessions: 'just a toothbrush' (l. 8). The narrator is more materialistic: he has an 'ansaphone' (l. 2) and is concerned about what he does and doesn't own. It is interesting that the car in which he committed his crime 'was hired' (l. 5). The hitcher talks poetically about the breeze in his hair; the narrator uses slang: 'I let him have it' (l. 11), 'Stitch that' (l. 24). He borrows phrases from the weather forecast ('The outlook for the day was moderate to fair', l. 23), which suggests he doesn't have the imagination to entertain independent thoughts or to empathise with his victim.

## Ideas to consider

* Both the narrator and the man he attacks are 'hitchers'. We know that the narrator 'thumbed a lift to where the car was parked' (l. 4). The man he then picks up is a casual traveller, with no set destination: 'He was following the sun to west from east' (l. 7). We cannot be sure which man is the 'Hitcher' of the title.

* Why does the narrator attack the hitchhiker? The attack does not seem premeditated. Perhaps it is because the hitcher has the freedom he wishes he himself could have. Could there be another reason?

* The poem seems to have a dark humour, but may contain more serious points too. Perhaps Armitage is commenting on meaningless violence in our society today.

### Key point

Bob Dylan, a singer–songwriter, wrote a song called 'Blowin' in the Wind'. It includes a number of rhetorical questions about life and war, and the chorus replies: 'The answer, my friend, is blowin' in the wind/The answer is blowin' in the wind'. First released in 1963, the song became something of an anthem for the hippie movement.

# Poem by poem
# Pre-1914
# Poetry Bank

## Biographies

**William Blake** (1757–1827) was the son of a London hosier. Instead of going to school, Blake was apprenticed to an engraver, learning how to illustrate books. He then studied at the Royal Academy of Arts. He married Catherine when he was 25; they had no children. He developed an interest in mysticism and, encouraged by visionary religious friends, began to publish poetry. In 1784 he set up his own print shop and began to publish his own works, including *Songs of Innocence and of Experience*. His work was only partially appreciated during his lifetime: he was thought of as gifted but mad.

**Robert Browning** (1812–89) was brought up by his sister in London and was mainly self-educated, roaming through his father's large library. He dropped out of university. He travelled in Europe and began to publish poetry (anonymously at first) and plays. In 1846 he famously eloped to Italy with the poet Elizabeth Barrett; they lived there until she died 15 years later. He set many of his poems in Europe. By the time he returned to England he was a famous and successful writer.

**John Clare** (1793–1864) was a rural labourer's son from Northamptonshire and grew up to be a hedge-setter. He always loved the countryside and was inspired to write about it, publishing his first

Robert Browning

poems in 1820. He married Martha Turner in the same year but never really got over his first love, Mary Joyce. His sadness overcame him and he was admitted to an asylum for the insane in 1837. Four years later he escaped and walked back to Mary, believing she was his wife. The rest of his life was spent in the asylum, writing poetry. He always insisted upon using his own language, dialect and grammar.

**Oliver Goldsmith** (1730–74) was born and brought up in Ireland, the son of a clergyman. His application to join the priesthood was turned down, so he turned to medicine, setting himself up as a physician without gaining a degree. He then began writing reviews for periodicals (literary magazines) and published more and more of his own works, although he never made much money. He also wrote plays, including the comic *She Stoops to Conquer*, which was a great success. He never married.

**Thomas Hardy** (1840–1928) was the son of a stonemason, and was encouraged by his mother to read throughout his childhood. He became an architect and worked in London, but continued to read voraciously and soon began to write his own novels. The success of his fourth published novel, *Far From the Madding Crowd*, in 1874, enabled him to give up architecture for writing and to marry Emma Gifford. Later on he gave up writing novels and turned to poetry, but continued to focus on the suffering in the world and the ironies of life. He married Florence Dugdale 2 years after Emma's death, when he was 74 and a famous writer.

**Gerard Manley Hopkins** (1844–89) grew up in Essex, the eldest of nine children. He won a scholarship to Oxford University and there became interested in exploring religion. He converted to Roman Catholicism and later joined the more extreme Jesuit organisation to train as a priest. At this stage he burned all his poems, believing that he could not serve God and write poetry at the same time. He only returned to writing in 1875, after an interval of 8 years. He tried to glorify God through his poetry, but he found life as a parish priest hard. Soon after a spell in Glasgow (where he wrote 'Inversnaid') he left the priesthood to become a professor at Dublin University. He died of typhoid.

**Ben Jonson** (1572/3–1637) never saw his own father, who died before he was born. He had an exciting early life, including fighting as a soldier in Flanders (where he killed an enemy champion in single combat). He also acted in a company of travelling players, where he killed a fellow actor in a duel and was subsequently imprisoned. He wrote many plays for the court (the first of which included Shakespeare in the cast), and poetry. James I admired his work and gave him a pension, which was a great honour. He was also given an honorary degree by Oxford University.

**William Shakespeare** (1564–1616) spent his childhood in Stratford-upon-Avon, where his father was a prominent local merchant. William probably attended the local grammar school. He married Anne Hathaway, who was 8 years his senior, and they had three children. It is not known when he began to write plays, but he was a member of the successful troupe The Lord Chamberlain's Men, which developed into London's leading company, based at the Globe Theatre. His sonnets were published in 1609; his many plays were not printed during his lifetime, simply performed. It was not until seven years after Shakespeare's death that the plays were first published.

TopFoto

Alfred Tennyson

**Alfred Tennyson** (1809–92) was the son of a rural priest. He went to Cambridge University and there wrote much poetry, even winning a prize. He travelled to Europe with his close friend Arthur Hallam, but Hallam drowned in 1833 and Tennyson wrote his famous poem 'In Memoriam' in his memory. His often melancholic and lyrical poetry became popular, and Queen Victoria made him poet laureate in 1850 (the same year in which he married) and, later, a baronet.

**Chidiock (Charles) Tichborne** (1558–86) was brought up in a Roman Catholic family. The Protestant Elizabeth I (having been excommunicated by the Pope) made Catholicism illegal, and Tichborne conspired in a Catholic plot to kill her. He was discovered and was executed by hanging. He was also disembowelled while still alive; when Elizabeth heard of this, she was so shocked that she banned the practice immediately. The 'Elegy' he wrote to his wife on the eve of his death is his only surviving poem. The *Anthology* is mistaken over his name: he was baptised Chidiock, not Charles.

**Walt Whitman** (1819–92) was born and brought up in New York. He received little schooling and worked, among other things, as a printer, politician and teacher. He travelled around America and contributed to various magazines while writing poetry. His work became widely admired. During the Civil War (1861–65) he volunteered as a hospital visitor; he later lived quietly in New Jersey. He never married and was probably homosexual.

**William Wordsworth** (1770–1850) was brought up in Cumbria, but his mother died when he was only 8 years old and his father when he was 13. He left Cambridge University to tour Europe and spent a period in Paris, where he supported the ideals of the French Revolution. He met the poet Coleridge in 1795; together they published *Lyrical Ballads*, a collection celebrating nature and self-expression that inspired other Romantic writers. Wordsworth married in 1802 and had five children, but he remained close to his sister, Dorothy. He settled in the Lake District and wrote much long, narrative poetry that proved popular. He became poet laureate in 1843.

**William Butler Yeats** (1865–1939), born in Ireland, was the eldest son of a famous painter. He himself began to study art, but gave it up in favour of literature, editing the work of other poets and writing his own. He was a committed Republican and supported movements to make Ireland independent from Britain — a theme that occurs in much of his poetry. He loved the beautiful and politically active Maud Gonne, but she refused him. He later married Georgie Hyde-Lees, a mystic, whose 'communicators' influenced his work. Yeats continued to be active in Irish politics throughout his life, becoming a senator in 1922. He was awarded the Nobel prize for literature in 1923.

W. B. Yeats

# 'On my first Sonne'

## What happens?

The poet is mourning the death of his dearly loved seven-year-old son. Ironically, he blames himself for the child's death: his 'sinne' (l. 2), or sin, was to have loved him too much. He considers a paradox: we mourn when we ought to rejoice that someone has escaped the burdens of the world and gone to Heaven. He resolves at the end never to love so intensely again, in order to avoid the same loss and grief.

### Glossary

**tho'wert** *(l. 3)* thou wert, or you were

**scap'd** *(l. 7)* escaped

**hence-forth** *(l. 11)* from now on

## Structure

The poem consists of six pairs of **rhyming couplets**. Most of the lines are **end-stopped**, so the rhymes chime softly through the poem. The lines are **iambic pentameters**, so there is a slow, even, natural rhythm.

## Language and imagery

Jonson writes in the **first person** to express his own personal emotions. The poem is spoken to the child, from father to son, and consequently feels very intimate.

The child was his 'right hand' (l. 1) because he was the eldest son (Jonson's heir) and because Jesus sat at God's right hand.

Jonson uses **banking imagery**. He says his son was 'lent' (l. 3) to him and that he, Jonson, paid back his creditor 'on the just day' (l. 4). As a Christian, Jonson believes that God creates all people, and he knows that he could never have expected to *own* something as precious as his son. He has returned him to God.

Jonson asks **rhetorical questions**. He wonders why he should 'lament' (l. 6) death when he really should 'envie' (l. 6) his son for going to a better place, i.e. Heaven. The world is full of 'fleshes rage' (l. 7) and 'miserie' (l. 8), while his son is able to 'Rest in soft peace' (l. 9).

**Pause for thought**

How do you think Jonson saw God?

The word 'poetry' comes from a Greek word meaning 'a thing made or created'. So Jonson — a writer more famous than Shakespeare in his day — is saying that his son is 'his best piece of poetrie' (l. 10), the best thing he ever created.

## Ideas to consider

* God is portrayed as a banker who lends humans to the world for a specified time. Likening birth and death to business transactions may sound callous, but Jonson seems in no doubt that his son really is in 'soft peace' with God, and is comforted by the thought.

* There is an interesting tension in the poem. If God 'lent' the child to Jonson, God must have been his creator. Yet Jonson also claims to have created the child, in the 'poetrie' image.

# 'The Song of the Old Mother'

## What happens?

As the Old Mother works from dawn to dusk she compares herself to rich and idle people. She has to do all the cleaning and cooking, while the young girls lie in bed all day and only worry if the wind disturbs their beautifully arranged hair. The old woman is tired and lonely and appears to resent her work.

### Glossary

**tress** *(l. 8)* a portion or lock of hair

## Structure

The poem is composed of five **rhyming couplets**, and so is a 'Song' — but not a very cheerful one. It is made up of one complete sentence, perhaps to suggest the never-ending nature of the woman's work. There are ten syllables in each line and ten lines in the poem, so it is a bit like a square, ten by ten. Perhaps this reflects the rigidity of her day.

## Language and imagery

The poem is written in the **first person**. Yeats takes on the **persona** of the old woman.

It is clear that the old woman works all day long, from 'dawn' (l. 1) 'Till stars are beginning to blink and peep' (l. 4). The stars are **personified** — although we don't get the impression that they peep down at her with any sympathy.

Her work is described in **bald**, **simple verbs**: 'kneel', 'blow', 'scrub', 'bake', 'sweep' (ll. 1–3). There is also the **imperative** 'must' (ll. 3 and 9). The verbs emphasise the harshness of her life.

In **contrast**, the young 'lie long and dream' (l. 5). The **alliteration** lengthens the 'l' sound, suggesting that they languish in idleness. There are strong comparisons between the old poor woman and the young rich girls. The young have nothing to do; the Old Mother 'must work' (l. 9).

Perhaps the most important of the old woman's tasks is to tend the fire. It is an effort: she has to 'kneel' to coax the 'seed' to life (l. 2). At the end of the day that 'seed' becomes 'feeble and cold' (l. 10). The dying fire is a **metaphor** for the old woman's life. She too is becoming 'feeble and cold', but the sad thing is that nobody seems to realise or care.

## Ideas to consider

* The title of the poem states that the woman is a 'Mother', yet it is unlikely that the 'young' are her own children. Perhaps her own offspring have grown up and left her all alone. Perhaps they have died. Or perhaps she is not a mother at all, but has somehow acquired the title 'Mother'. (If so, is that respectful or disrespectful?)

**Pause for thought**

> What is the old woman's relationship to the young people? Is she their servant?

# 'The Affliction of Margaret'

## What happens?

The poem is about the desperation of a mother to find news of her son, her 'only child' (l. 9), whom she has not heard from for seven years. She describes his happy childhood and how proud she was of him when he left home. Discounting the idea that he may simply be neglecting her, she worries about what may have happened to him — he could be ashamed to come home because he is impoverished, or he

### Glossary

**affliction** pain, misery
**beguiled** (l. 11) deluded, cheated
**beauteous to behold** (l. 16) beautiful to look at
**intercourse** (l. 59) communication

could even be imprisoned or drowned. If he is dead, she reasons that there cannot be communication between the living and dead, or she would have heard from him. Finally the poem goes full circle and ends as it began, with a plea for news of the son.

## Structure

The poem consists of eleven equal stanzas of seven lines. There is a strict **rhyme scheme** of ABABCCC in each one. The rhymes in the last three lines are often extremely poignant. (Look again at stanzas 4, 7 and 11.)

## Language and imagery

The poem is written in the **first person**: Wordsworth is taking on the **persona** of Margaret. It is interesting that we know *her* name but never learn the name of the son.

Margaret uses fairly formal language, which suggests she is educated. She uses the familiar 'thou' instead of 'you' (like the French 'tu'), as was usual 200 years ago.

 **Pause for thought**

Is Margaret's impression of her son accurate, or is she deceiving herself (and us)?

'The very shadows of the clouds
Have power to shake me as they pass'

Margaret has numerous ideas about why she has not heard from her son, ranging from simple 'Neglect' (l. 29) to fears that he's been 'summon'd to the Deep' (l. 54) or has died in some other way.

The seventh stanza (ll. 43–49) contains the most complex language and imagery. The 'fowls of Heaven' are birds. Margaret is saying that birds can fly far and wide, aided by the winds ('blasts of Heaven'); *because* they can fly they can quickly find their 'delight' — or whatever it is they are searching for. In contrast, humans are tied down to 'land and sea' and so do not have the freedom of birds. Therefore all Margaret can do is wish for her son to come home and pray that he is comforted, wherever he is — although she recognises this is a 'vain' hope. The stanza expresses how frustrated Margaret feels that she is powerless to find her son.

## Ideas to consider

* There is a sense of mystery about Margaret's son. The reader doesn't know his fate; we are left to speculate, like Margaret.
* Margaret is clearly proud of her son: 'He was among the prime in worth' (l. 15). How much can we believe her claims?

# 'The Little Boy Lost'/'The Little Boy Found'

## What happens?

In the first of this pair of poems a child wanders alone on a dark night through dangerous boggy ground. He seems to be abandoned by his father. In the second poem a lost child is returned by God to his distraught mother. (We assume that it is the same child.)

### Glossary

**mire** *(LBL, l. 7)* swampy ground, bog

**vapour** *(LBL, l. 8)* mist

**dale** *(LBF, l. 7)* valley

## Structure

Each poem is composed of two **quatrains**, and both rhyme ABCB. They seem like nursery rhymes — on the surface.

## Language and imagery

The first poem begins in the **first person** as we hear the boy's pleas to his father not to abandon him. This plunges the reader straight into a dramatic and dangerous situation and we sympathise with the boy, although we are not sure whether the father has deliberately abandoned the child or whether the boy has simply wandered away. Blake then switches to the **third person**: we are told what happens by an omniscient (all-knowing) narrator.

There is a mysterious reference to 'vapour' (LBL, l. 8). Perhaps the child was lost in the mist — or was he following it (as Blake suggests in the engraving illustrating the poem)? The second poem seems to confirm this: the child is 'Led by the wand'ring light' (LBF, l. 2), but we are not told exactly what this light is, and whether it is good or evil.

'The Little Boy Lost' illustration from *Songs of Innocence and of Experience*

Fitzwilliam Museum, University of Cambridge, UK/Bridgeman Art Library

## Ideas to consider

* Blake makes us question the role of a father. We are horrified in the first poem when the father abandons his child, and in such a dangerous place. Yet in the second poem God appears in human form, 'like his father' (l. 4), and leads the boy to safety. Christians call God 'Our Father'.

We also consider the role of the mother. She was obviously desperate to find her child, as she is 'in sorrow pale' (LBF, l. 7), but she was looking in the wrong place, 'the lonely dale' (LBF, l. 7). She would not have found him without God's help.

## Key point

Blake was an illustrator, poet and mystic. These poems come from *The Songs of Innocence and of Experience*. Deceptively simple poems, they were written apparently for children, but they have much Christian symbolism and important messages for adults too.

## Pause for thought

What do the child, mother and father represent? What do the 'vapour' and the 'wand'ring light' symbolise? What messages was Blake trying to convey through the poems?

# 'Tichborne's Elegy'

## What happens?

In the poem, Tichborne laments his premature death. He uses a number of comparisons and images to show that his life is wasted and is over too early.

## Structure

The poem consists of three equal stanzas of six lines, each with a **refrain**. There is an ABABCC rhyme scheme and a regular iambic rhythm, which shows remarkable control for someone who was due to die in the morning. Perhaps concentrating on writing an ordered poem helped to keep Tichborne calm.

## Glossary

**cares** *(l. 1)* worries

**tares** *(l. 3)* vetch, a weed in corn

**shade** *(l. 14)* here, a ghost

**glass** *(l. 17)* an hourglass (see the illustration above the poem in the *Anthology*)

## Language and imagery

The poem is, of course, in the **first person**. (It is significant that, of all the poems in the *Anthology*, this one was never meant for publication. It contains Tichborne's intimate thoughts, meant only for his wife.)

Each line is a **balanced statement**. The first half of the line sets up an image; the second, after the **caesura**, shows how that image, in Tichborne's situation, is turned on its head. For example, he should be in his 'prime of youth' but is instead in the winter of his life, with a cold 'frost of cares' (l. 1); the earth he 'trod' is about to be his 'tomb' (l. 15). 'But' is used a lot to mark the contrast and here means 'only'.

## Pause for thought

Which contrasting metaphors do you feel are most effective?

Tichborne uses various **metaphors** to illustrate his state. For instance, the first stanza contains food imagery ('feast of joy … dish of pain': l. 2) and farming imagery ('crop of corn … field of tares': l. 3). This last metaphor is interesting, as Jesus uses a similar image in a parable.

The refrain is a sort of **paradox**: he still lives, but his life is essentially over.

## Ideas to consider

* Tichborne uses 'My' and 'I' frequently. Do you think this shows introspection or selfishness? (He doesn't appear to think of his loved ones at all.)

> **Key point**
>
> Tichborne, a Roman Catholic, was sentenced to death for having joined a plot to kill Elizabeth I. He was only 28 years old. On the night before his execution, he wrote to his wife Agnes, enclosing this poem.

# 'The Man He Killed'

## What happens?

The poet tells an unidentified listener about a man he killed. He says that in any other circumstance he and the man would have been friends and shared a drink. Because they met in wartime, they happened to be enemies and shot each other.

## Structure

The poem consists of five **quatrains**, each rhyming ABAB. The lines are short (lines 1, 2 and 4 contain six syllables; line 3 has eight) and so the poem appears very simple. Perhaps the deceptively simple form reinforces the simple message.

## Language and imagery

The poem is written in the **first person**: Hardy takes on the **persona** of the soldier. The poem is written within speech marks, so either the soldier is narrating what happened to

## Glossary

**nipperkin** (l. 4) a small measure (less than half a pint) for wine, ale, etc.
**ranged** (l. 5) arranged (in lines)
**'list** (l. 13) enlist, join the army
**traps** (l. 15) trappings, possessions, stuff

> **Key point**
>
> Hardy wrote this poem during the second Boer War (1899–1902). The poem is not just about that war, however — it could be about *any* war.

someone else or the speech marks reinforce the fact that this is a persona — not the poet reflecting to himself, but someone talking aloud, relating his experience to an audience (perhaps the listening poet).

The poem starts in the **conditional** tense, 'Had he and I but met' (or '*If* we had met'). We get the feeling that the soldier means 'If only'; right from the start there is an element of doubt.

The first stanza **contrasts** with the second. Instead of sharing a drink together casually, the two soldiers were arranged in formal lines and obliged to shoot each other. The simple, one-syllable words make lines 7–8 bald and stark.

In the third stanza, the soldier searches for a reason *why* he killed his 'foe' (l. 10). The **repetition** of 'because' and the use of 'Just so... of course.../That's clear enough' (ll. 11–12) suggest that he himself is unconvinced. It is **ironic** that he can't explain why the man had to die.

The fourth stanza highlights the similarities between the men. Both enlisted casually, 'Off-hand like' (l. 14), because they were out of work and had sold all their things.

### Ideas to consider

* Why is the soldier telling the tale? Do you think he needs to get it off his chest? Does he feel guilty for killing a fellow who would have been a friend if they had met in any other circumstance (ll.18–20)?
* What is Hardy's attitude to war? Does he really think it is 'quaint and curious' (l. 17), or is that an ironic understatement?

# 'Patrolling Barnegat'

## What happens?

The poem is set on a dark, stormy night. The narrator is walking along the beach alone and he finds it hard to make out exactly what he can see through the wild weather. He wonders if he spies a wreck; we, like the poet, are never sure.

**Key point**

Barnegat is a beach in New Jersey, USA, in what is today called Ocean County. It is famous for sailing.

## Structure

The poem consists of 14 lines and is therefore a **sonnet**, but a very unusual one. Sonnets are often ordered pieces about love or loss: this one is confused and chaotic. There is only one full stop, right at the end, but even then the poem is not a complete sentence because there is no main verb. It is simply a list of clauses piled together. The lack of order in the poetry echoes the wild scenes it describes.

## Language and imagery

The poem is apparently written in the **first person** but the narrator never refers to himself (or herself) directly. In fact there are no personal pronouns. This both distances the reader from the reporter, making us concentrate on the storm, and alienates us, so *we* feel alone too.

Every line ends with a verb ending in '–ing', a **present participle**. This helps to create pace in the poem as we sense we are being rushed along, and also sets up a mysterious echoing sound-track.

The poet uses **personification** to create an atmosphere of disorder and fear. The gale is 'muttering' (l. 2), the waves are 'careering' (l. 5), for example. This effect is heightened by using **military imagery**: the 'death-wind' is 'breasting' (l. 7) and 'advancing' (l. 8) as if it were going into battle. There is a real sense of danger.

### Pause for thought

Why do you think Whitman never allows us to be sure about whether there was a wreck? Do you think the poem is more effective *because* we are not sure?

The poet refers to the 'Waves, air, midnight' as a 'trinity' (ll. 4 and 14), which is perhaps an ironic link to the Christian trinity of God the Father, Son and Holy Ghost. The violent trinity in the poem seems closer to the devil than to God — especially with the reference to 'demoniac laughter' (l. 3). Perhaps the poet is questioning who has power over the elements: God, or a more evil force.

There is a lot of **alliteration** in the poem to link ideas together and create sound effects, such as in line 6 where the repeated 's' sounds reflect the hissing sounds of the snow storm.

## Ideas to consider

* Does the narrator really see a 'wreck' and 'red signal' (l. 9) out at sea, or is it an optical illusion caused by the storm?
* If so, is the wreck the cause of the 'dim, weird forms' (l. 13) that appear to struggle in the water? If not, what could those forms be?

# 'Sonnet 130'

## What happens?

This is one of over 150 sonnets written by Shakespeare. Through it he both mocks other writers of sonnets who use clichés in their writing and praises his own lover.

He looks at the techniques of other poets, who praise their lovers by making romantic but wildly exaggerated comparisons (such as comparing lips with coral or voices with music), and vows to tell the truth about his own lover. The final

couplet shows that although he has been honest in describing her, he still knows her to be 'rare' and special — perhaps more so than other women who have 'false' comparisons made about them.

## Structure

The sonnet is tightly structured. It has a **precise rhyme scheme** of ABAB CDCD EFEF GG, a pattern so often used by Shakespeare that it has become known as a 'Shakespearean sonnet'. It is made up of **iambic pentameters**, so has a gentle rhythm.

## Glossary

**mistress** *(l. 1)* lover (not necessarily a woman having an affair)

**dun** *(l. 3)* dull greyish brown

**damask rose** *(l. 5)* a rose coloured velvety pink

**reeks** *(l. 8)* smells (but not necessarily unpleasantly)

**belied** *(l. 14)* given a false idea of

## Language and imagery

The poem is written in the **first person**, but that does not necessarily mean that Shakespeare was in love: he wrote for his patron, the Earl of Southampton.

The first line **surprises** us. In a typical love poem, we may expect a lover's eyes to 'shine brighter than the sun', but Shakespeare deliberately turns this stereotypical **simile** on its head: he claims his lover's eyes are 'nothing like the sun'.

The poem continues, systematically, to consider other similes often used by lovers — and to reject them. In total eight comparisons are explored. The poet is expressing his own true love by rejecting false clichés.

The similes develop as the poem goes on. Lines 1–4 each focus on one of the woman's features (her eyes, lips, breasts and hair). However, warming to his theme, Shakespeare expands his argument by using two lines per feature in lines 5–12 (her cheeks, breath, voice and movement).

## Pause for thought

**Do you think that Shakespeare was a more genuine lover than the poets who praised their mistresses with wildly exaggerated images?**

The final **rhyming couplet** contains the main message of the poem. His exclamation, 'by heaven' (l. 13), is used to emphasise his point as some people might say 'God!' today, but it could also suggest he is thankful for his 'rare' love. He believes her to be more special to him than any woman 'belied with false compare', or mocked by untrue comparisons.

## Ideas to consider

* The poem is focused solely on the woman's appearance. Does this suggest that Shakespeare thought that looks were everything, or does his description of her hint at what she was like as a person too?

# 'My Last Duchess'

## What happens?

The Duke is showing a guest a picture of his former wife, the last Duchess, painted by a famous artist. It is a private picture, hidden behind a curtain. The Duke tells the listener about his former wife — how she was easily flattered and loved attention. He resents the fact that she did not value his 'gift of a nine-hundred-years-old name' (l. 33) any more than little day-to-day pleasures she enjoyed, and he was too proud to 'stoop' (l. 43) to tell her off. Finally he 'gave commands' (l. 45) and — we assume — had her murdered. It is only at the end of the poem that we realise the person he is talking to is the envoy from a Count, the father of the Duke's bride-to-be. The Duke claims not to be interested in his new wife's dowry, but perhaps we wonder.

### Glossary

**mantle** *(l. 16)* loose, sleeveless cloak

**munificence** *(l. 49)* generosity

**dowry** *(l. 51)* money paid to a bridegroom by a bride's father

## Structure

The poem consists of pairs of **rhyming couplets** (or **heroic couplets**). The rhymes are disguised because most lines use **enjambement**, so the poem sounds more like natural speech. It is written in **iambic pentameters**, which also contribute to the natural style.

## Language and imagery

The poem is a **dramatic monologue**. We take on the role of the listener along with the Count's envoy, and as we do so we gradually work out the narrative. The words seem very convincing, helped particularly by the Duke's pauses and hesitations (e.g. l. 22, ll. 31–32).

Although only one character speaks, we learn much about the Duke and the Duchess, and something about the artist Frà Pandolf and the Count's envoy. We are not told everything directly: we **infer** details, or read between the lines. For example, we are not told for certain what relationship the Duchess had with the artist or how the Duchess behaved in front of her husband. We know the Duke is a man used to being obeyed, and he tells us: 'I gave commands;/Then all smiles stopped together' (ll. 45–46). This is a **euphemism**, enabling the Duke to avoid stating outright that the Duchess died, which is typical of the **ambiguity** present in the poem.

**Pause for thought**

Is the statue as valuable to the Duke as the painting of his last wife? If so, will the Duke value his new wife in the same heartless way?

**Key point**

Ferrara is in what is now northern Italy. It used to be an independent state, governed by a rich and powerful duke. In this poem, Browning takes on the persona of an imagined Duke of Ferrara.

The Duke appears to be **critical**: 'She had/A heart — how shall I say? — too soon made glad' (ll. 21–22). He also seems **proud** (he highlights his family name, and would not 'stoop'), **heartless** (he shows no regret for his wife's death), **confident** (he tells the story to the envoy, apparently without fearing that it could jeopardise his next marriage), and **cold** (he seems to appreciate works of art more than people).

## Ideas to consider

* It is significant that the poem ends as it began, with the Duke showing the envoy a piece from his art collection. Yet while the first piece was a portrait of his dead wife, the second is a bronze statue of Neptune 'Taming a sea-horse' (l. 55). Perhaps this suggests that the Duke likes to tame people too?
* Do you have any sympathy with the Duke? And the Duchess?
* With what message will the envoy return to the Count?

# 'The Laboratory'

## What happens?

It is not immediately clear who is speaking in this **dramatic monologue** — but clues gradually suggest that it is a rich woman, a courtier who often dances 'at the King's' (l. 12). She seems so jealous of her rival that she is prepared to kill her, which is why the monologue takes place in an alchemist's. She is watching him as he creates a poison that she will use to murder the woman who has 'ensnared' (l. 30) the man she herself loves. She is so delighted with the result that she is prepared to pay the alchemist with all her jewels and gold.

## Structure

The poem consists of twelve stanzas (each numbered, a little like chapters in a novel). Each stanza is made up of two **rhyming couplets** (so the rhyme scheme is AABB), perhaps because the poet wanted to suggest the story is ancient or historic.

### Glossary

**Ancien Régime** French for 'old rule'; specifically, the system of government in France before the Revolution of 1789.

**prithee** (l. 4) please

**brave** (l. 14) mighty, splendid, admirable

**phial** (l. 15) a small glass bottle, usually used for medicine

**filigree** (l. 20) delicate metalwork (often in a precious metal)

**minion** (l. 29) a favourite child, servant or girl

## Language and imagery

Because the poem is a monologue, it is written in the **present tense** and so contains drama and tension. We are drawn into the narrative and wonder what will happen.

It contains **archaic phrases** (such as 'prithee' and 'minion') to anchor the story in the past, as if it is a fairy tale. Yet there is a tension between the historical feel of the poem and the immediacy of the story that unfolds.

The speaker reveals a lot about herself. For instance, she is not meek, as her lover and rival assume her to be when they imagine she is in the 'drear/Empty church' (ll. 7–8), but **vengeful** and **bitter**. She is **curious** — she wants to know about the ingredients of the poisons (stanza 4). She is also **cautious**: she wears a mask throughout and ensures that the alchemist brushes the dust off before she grants him a final kiss (stanza 12).

**Alliteration** is used in places to emphasise and link ideas, such as 'Pound at thy powder' (l. 10) and 'Brand, burn up, bite into its grace' (l. 39). The harsh 'p' and 'b' sounds help stress the woman's anger, as if she is spitting out the words.

## Ideas to consider

* Not everything is solved for us. For example, we know very little about the woman's lover and why she is prepared to go to such lengths to keep him for herself. And why are *two* women (Pauline and Elise) mentioned in stanza 6, when the woman seems to concentrate on *one* rival throughout the rest of the poem?
* The subtitle to the poem is 'Ancien Régime', as if the writer wants to suggest that the subject of the poem is in the past. Yet many of the themes are relevant today — including jealousy, vengefulness, and the lengths people (like the alchemist) will go to for money.

> **Key point**
>
> The French court was seen as particularly decadent, which is one factor that led to the Revolution. Browning reflects this decadence in the poem.

# 'Ulysses'

## What happens?

1 Tennyson sets his poem many years after Ulysses' previous adventures, when Ulysses and his wife have become 'aged' (l. 3). He feels 'idle' (l. 1) and resentful of his people, whom he calls a 'savage race' (l. 4) and who do not respect him ('know not me': l. 5).

2 For these reasons he decides to travel again, to get the most out of the rest of his life. He is proud of his fame ('I am become a name': l. 11). He wishes

to maximise the time that remains to him ('everyhour…saved/From…eternal silence': ll. 26–27), to make new discoveries and 'follow knowledge' (l. 31).

3 He arranges to hand over rule of Ithaca to his 'Well-loved' (l. 35) son, Telemachus, whom he sees as more suited to the task than he is.

4 Finally he prepares his ship with his faithful mariners. They are all aware that this is likely to be their final voyage and that they will never return, but Ulysses hopes 'Some work of noble note, may yet be done' (l. 52). He encourages his men, reminding them that although they are old and weak, they are 'strong in will' (l. 69) and will not give up.

## Glossary

**mete** *(l. 3)* allot, hand out
**lees** *(l. 7)* dregs
**Hyades** *(l. 10)* a cluster of stars — reputedly a sign of rain
**meet** *(l. 42)* correct, fitting
**gulfs** *(l. 62)* waters spilling off the edge of the world (when it was believed the world was flat)
**Happy Isles** *(l. 63)* Elysium, the home for heroes after death
**Achilles** *(l. 64)* Ulysses' friend, killed at Troy.

## Structure

The poem consists of four sections (like paragraphs), each dealing with a different part of Ulysses' preparations to set sail again. Throughout, Tennyson uses **iambic pentameters**. These sound like natural speech, although sometimes Tennyson uses the iambic rhythm to great effect. The final line has a stress on all the key words and is a strong rallying cry to the mariners: 'To <u>strive</u>, to <u>seek</u>, to <u>find</u>, and <u>not</u> to <u>yield</u>'.

## Language and imagery

The poem is a **dramatic monologue**. The language is fitting for a great leader. Ulysses uses balanced sentences, such as 'I cannot rest from travel: I will drink/Life to the lees' (ll. 6–7) and 'He works his work, I mine' (l .43), which are memorable.

We learn much about Ulysses. He is **old**, with a 'gray spirit' (l. 30); but his statement, 'I am a part of all that I have met' (l. 18), shows his awareness that **all experiences shape us** in some way. He is **realistic**, aware that Telemachus will rule Ithaca better than he has done through 'slow prudence' (l. 36). Yet he is also **impatient** to be off, and looks to the future. He has strong bonds to his loyal sailors.

He often uses imagery. For example, there is a **metaphor** of himself as a metal tool or armour gaining 'rust' when he wishes to 'shine in use' (l. 23).

> **Key point**
>
> Another name for Ulysses is Odysseus. He was a hero during the Trojan Wars (smuggling soldiers into Troy inside the 'gift' of a wooden horse was his idea). He then experienced many adventures in the course of his return home to Ithaca. On his arrival he found his wife beset by many suitors who all believed him to be dead.

## Ideas to consider

* The poem encourages people not to give up and to make the most of their lives.
* Do you admire Ulysses for his enthusiasm and strength of purpose, or criticise him for leaving his country and its problems to Telemachus? (And what about his wife?)
* The poem was written after the death of Tennyson's close friend, Arthur Hallam. Perhaps writing the poem helped give Tennyson the will to pick up his life again and carry on.

# 'The Village Schoolmaster'

## What happens?

The poem describes a schoolmaster in a small rural school. It describes his attitude to his pupils — and theirs to him — and then outlines his accomplishments. He was skilled in practical subjects like writing and sums and measuring land. He could debate with the parson and use long, impressive words, all of which amazed the villagers.

### Glossary

**furze** *(l. 2)* gorse, a heathland shrub with yellow flowers
**gay** *(l. 2)* cheerful
**boding** *(l. 7)* expectant, waiting
**cipher** *(l. 16)* do arithmetic
**presage** *(l. 17)* predict
**gauge** *(l. 18)* estimate the area of a piece of land

## Structure

The poem is written in **rhyming couplets**. Most are **end-stopped** so the rhymes are obvious, and they contribute to the light, upbeat tone of the poem. The lines are **iambic pentameters** and so sound like natural speech.

## Language and imagery

The poem is written in the **first person**, but we have no idea who the speaker is. We only know that he knew the village and its inhabitants well.

The schoolmaster was good at his job. The poet states he was 'skilled to rule' (l. 3), 'kind' (l. 13) and had a great 'love...[of] learning' (l. 14). This suggests he was an ideal teacher.

However, we also learn that the schoolmaster could be 'severe...and stern' (l. 5); and

### Key point

The poem in the *Anthology* is an extract from a much longer poem, *The Deserted Village*, based on a village in Ireland. In it Goldsmith describes a village deserted due to financial hardship and looks back to an idealised past.

(arguably a greater criticism) when debating with the parson he used 'words of learned length and thundering sound' (l. 21) just for the sake of impressing his audience. He was obviously concerned with keeping up his educated appearance.

### Pause for thought

**The poet seems both to admire the school-master and to mock him. Which idea do you think comes across more strongly?**

We also learn a lot about the villagers. The fact that the small rural school-house is called a 'mansion' (l. 3) is ironic, but it also suggests that the villagers lived in tiny dwellings. They had little education, being easily impressed by the school-master's learning: 'The village all declared how much he knew' (l. 15). It seems even to have been the subject of local gossip — 'the story ran that he could gauge' (l. 18). They seem to have been proud of their schoolmaster.

### Ideas to consider

* Goldsmith uses irony to great effect. Having said that the villagers admired all the schoolmaster knew, he undercuts this by saying, "Twas certain he could write, and cipher too' (l. 16) — rather basic skills.
* Goldsmith presents us with a community in which the parson and the school-master are superior to everyone else: social divisions are fixed. However, perhaps the financial crisis that caused the village to be deserted was partly a result of the rigid class structure.

# 'The Eagle'

## What happens?

In this brief poem (Tennyson subtitled it 'A Fragment') we see the world from an eagle's eye view. The powerful bird is poised on the edge of a high cliff, watching for prey; when he sees it he swoops down to the sea like a thunder-bolt to claim it.

## Structure

The poem consists of two **triplets** (or stanzas of three lines rhyming together). We can perhaps see the tight, pared-down structure as conveying something of the gaunt, forceful bird.

David Macias/SPL

## Language and imagery

The poem is written in the **present tense**, which adds tension and drama.

The eagle is **personified**. He has 'hands' (l. 1), and as he 'stands' (l. 3) on his crag, he 'watches' (l. 5) intently. He reminds us of a king or army general surveying the scene. There is a sense that he is the master.

The use of **pronouns** in the poem is interesting. The eagle is given ownership over 'his mountain walls' (l. 5); and the sea 'beneath him crawls' (l. 4) almost as if it were subservient to him. This increases the sense of majesty and power.

The **imagery** in the poem is striking. The eagle is placed in the centre of things, 'Ring'd with the azure world' (l. 3), as if everything revolves around him. The sea is 'wrinkled' (l. 4) below him, a vivid adjective to describe the far-away waves. The final **simile** is also forceful: the eagle falls 'like a thunderbolt' (l. 6). This gives him huge power and hints at the destruction of his prey.

There is **alliteration** in the poem: 'He clasps the crag with crookèd hands' and 'lonely lands' (ll. 1–2). This links ideas and further 'tightens' the poem.

## Ideas to consider

* It is interesting that although Tennyson gave the eagle characteristics of a powerful man, mankind is not mentioned in the poem. (Are the 'lonely lands' (l. 2) places without humans or without any life at all?) Perhaps there is a message here: Tennyson may be hinting that humans are not as all-powerful as they would like to believe.

* We are given the eagle's point of view. He considers himself strong, mighty and in control: he has power over life and death.

# 'Inversnaid'

## What happens?

Hopkins describes a favourite scene in the Highlands. He follows the path of a burn as it falls over a small waterfall and down a mountain to a lake, then focuses in (like a cinematic shot) on some froth being spun round on the fast-moving water. In the third stanza he describes the burn's banks and surroundings. The final stanza is a passionate plea to people to conserve such areas 'Of wet and of wildness' (l. 14) — a message that is even more important today than when Hopkins wrote 'Inversnaid'.

## Structure

The poem consists of four equal stanzas of four lines. Each stanza is made up of two **rhyming couplets**, rhyming AABB. This scheme creates a bouncing pace,

reminiscent of the quick-flowing water. The lines are on average eight syllables long; the variation perhaps suggests the random path of the water.

## Language and imagery

The poem is in the **present tense**. Hopkins describes the scene in such detail that he seems to be personally pointing different features out to us — especially as the first word is 'This'. We are drawn into the poem.

Hopkins typically uses language in an original and imaginative way. He invents **compound words** by joining together two words that are not usually associated with each other, like 'rollrock' (l. 2) and 'windpuff' (l. 5). He also creates **portmanteau words** like 'twindles' (l. 6), which seems to be a mixture of 'twists', 'twitches' and 'dwindles'. These are all words which would make very little sense outside the poem but seem perfect for what Hopkins is describing.

There is a sort of **extended metaphor** in the first stanza: the burn is likened to a horse, not only because of its 'horseback brown' colour (l. 1) — from the peat the water passes through on the moors — but because it seems to be 'roaring down' a 'highroad' (l. 2), 'home' (l. 4) to the lake, its 'fleece' (l. 3) (or mane) flying.

The language of the second stanza is more complex. Hopkins describes a little ball of fawn-coloured froth on the surface of the water being tossed over a dark whirlpool. (The pool is dark because it is in the shadow of the fells.) The pool could be an image of 'Despair' (like Hell), or maybe it is so dark that Despair itself could be drowning in it.

Hopkins uses frequent **alliteration** and **consonance** in the poem to great effect. For example, the 'r' sounds in 'ro̱llro̱ck highṟoad ṟoaring down' (l. 2) suggest the rushing pace of the stream, while there are heavy 'd' sounds in 'rouṉds and rouṉds Despair to ḏrowning' (l. 8). Note the echoing **assonance** too, such as 'ro̱llrock highro̱ad ro̱aring do̱wn', which further intensify the sound effects in the poem.

 **Pause for thought**

> To whom might Hopkins have wanted to deliver his message?

### Glossary

**Inversnaid** a place in the Highlands of Scotland, overlooking Loch Lomond

**burn** (l. 1) small stream

**flutes** (l. 4) frills, becomes frilly

**degged** (l. 9) sprinkled (a northern dialect word)

**braes** (l. 10) steep banks, hillsides

**flitches** (l. 11) usually cuts from a tree; here, ragged tufts

**ash** (l. 12) a rowan tree, which has orange-red berries

**bereft** (l. 13) robbed, deprived, bereaved

The tone changes in the final stanza. Hopkins uses the word 'bereft' (l. 13) to suggest that the loss of such environments would be like the death of a loved one for us. He poses a **rhetorical question** to make us think about the importance of natural environments.

## Ideas to consider

* It is interesting that the light puff of froth *escapes* the whirlpool in stanza 2. Perhaps Hopkins, a fervent Christian, is suggesting that Despair is not inevitable — that if one is 'light' enough through faith in God, one will 'float' over troubles.
* The final plea for the conservation of wild places contains **rhetorical devices** like **repetition** and **alliteration** and the use of a **passive verb**, 'Let them be left' (l. 14), almost like a politician's speech.

# 'Sonnet'

## What happens?

The poem is a simple expression of the poet's fondness for summer. He describes the clouds, the flowers, the birds and the insects.

## Glossary

**Mare blobs** *(l. 4)* marsh marigolds

**drain** *(l. 4)* gully at the bottom of the meadow for excess water

**flag** *(l. 8)* wild iris

## Structure

The poem is, of course, a sonnet, consisting of seven **rhyming couplets**. Sonnets are a traditional form for love poetry. Here Clare is expressing his love not for a woman, but for a season and a landscape.

There is no punctuation at all in the poem, which emphasises its simplicity.

## Language and imagery

In a sense the poet is **like a film director**. He begins with a wide-angle lens and describes the clouds, then a distant view of the marsh marigolds. They are so distant that he doesn't see them individually, but as a golden stain on the 'meadow drain' (l. 4). He then zooms in on details such as the Moor Hen, and finally he gives us a close-up of the insects. The effect is to give us a whole panorama of the scene and encourage us to appreciate every detail.

The language used is very **simple**, almost childlike. There is **repetition** of 'I love' and adjectives such as 'clear', and most of the words are of one syllable. It is as if the poet did not want to tarnish his vision with anything more complex.

The poem **appeals to our senses**. For example, we *see* the white and gold flowers, *hear* the 'rustle' (l. 6) of the reeds, *feel* the 'winds' (l. 12) and *smell* the 'hay grass' (l. 11).

The poet uses a **range of imagery**. Summer itself is **personified** as a cheery person 'beaming forth' (l. 1), while there is a **mixed metaphor** to describe the clouds: they are both 'white wool sack[s]' and ships in full sail (l. 2).

**Alliteration** is used to link ideas and create sound effects. Here you can hear the wind: 'Where reed clumps rustle like a wind shook wood' (l. 6).

## Ideas to consider

* The poem glorifies the scene that Clare portrays. It is interesting that he highlights the colours white and gold, to suggest a majestic or even religious atmosphere. Do you think that, by extension, Clare is glorifying *all* of nature?
* Clare had been through a personal crisis just before he wrote this poem. How do you think that writing the 'Sonnet' may have helped him?

# Themes

As you read this section, ask yourself:
- ➢ What are the most important themes in Duffy's poetry?
- ➢ What are the most important themes in Armitage's poetry?
- ➢ What themes do they share — and how do they treat these themes?

When we talk about themes in poetry, we mean ideas that recur in a poet's work. They are usually ideas that the poet feels are important and wants to explore in some way. They can be triggered by many things: perhaps a memory, or something the poet has experienced, or the world around them. The poet returns to these ideas and looks at them from different angles in different poems. Often themes are interrelated: Duffy, for example, looks at both childhood and memory.

It is difficult to define the themes of a particular poet precisely. Different people will have different readings of poems, so interpretation has to be taken into account. The general drift of a theme is usually clear, although the specific titles people give to each theme may be different.

## Duffy

### Women

Duffy is interested in both real women ('Anne Hathaway' and 'Salome') and fictional women ('Havisham' and 'Elvis's Twin Sister'). She focuses on these characters because previously they have been overshadowed by men in the public consciousness. Shakespeare is usually seen as more important than his wife, Anne; St John the Baptist is revered whereas Salome is effectively seen as his murderer. In literature, the reader of *Great Expectations* is more interested in the fortunes of Pip than those of Miss Havisham. Duffy asks us to look at these women whom we had ignored before and imagine what it must have been like to be them. Elvis never had a twin sister — the character is invented by Duffy — but if he had had one, shut away in a convent, she would never have eclipsed her brother.

Other women are presented in the *Anthology*'s selection of Duffy's poetry. Duffy's youthful mother appears in 'Before You Were Mine'. It is possible that both the parent and the grown-up child featured in 'We Remember Your Childhood

Well' are women — the genders of these characters are disguised. Perhaps, too, the young people in 'Education for Leisure' and 'Stealing' are young women. We cannot tell: it may be that the theme of women unites all of the poems you are studying.

## Memory

Memory is another theme that may unite all Duffy's poems in the *Anthology*. We are shown that some memories are valuable. Anne Hathaway is sustained by memories of making love to Shakespeare: 'I hold him in the casket of my head' ('Anne Hathaway'). Elvis's twin remembers a solitary past —'Long time since I walked/down Lonely Street' ('Elvis's Twin Sister') — which she compares to a present filled with companions (so the memory of lonely times is valuable as it makes her grateful for her life now). 'Before You Were Mine' deals with two layers of precious memories: Duffy's memories of herself as a child with her mother ('I remember my hands in those high-heeled red shoes') and her mother's memories of her youth as retold to (or imagined by) Duffy.

Yet memories can also be painful. Miss Havisham's sour memories poison her life: 'Spinster. I stink and remember' ('Havisham'). The child in 'We Remember Your Childhood Well' is haunted by memories of many unhappy times — times which the parent(s) either dismiss, or remember in a different way. There is a touch of poignant humour in the fact that Salome can't remember the name of the man sharing her bed, which underlines the intrinsic sadness of her life: 'What was his name? Peter?/Simon? Andrew? John?' ('Salome').

Significantly, the character in 'Stealing' talks only of memories of things they've stolen, while the character in 'Education for Leisure' speaks mainly in the present tense and is almost devoid of memory (the only thing remembered is that 'We did [Shakespeare] at school'). Perhaps Duffy denied these two unstable characters a developed memory to emphasise the importance of memories in maintaining balance in our lives.

## Parents and children

Many of the women featured in the selection are mothers and all, of course, are someone's daughter, so Duffy's interest in writing about women naturally extends to exploring childhood and the relationship between parents and children. However, she does not present us with cosy, loving images. The most affectionate portrayal is that shown in 'Before You Were Mine', where Duffy describes her own mother's happy, carefree life before Duffy was born — with the implication that once she became a mother, life lost its sparkle.

Duffy focuses on relationships that failed. 'We Remember Your Childhood Well' features an embittered situation, with the repeated denials of the parent(s) and the lack of trust shown by their child. In two of the poems ('Education for

Leisure' and 'Stealing') we are interested in the absence of a parental figure. We wonder what the narrators' relationships with their parents had been like to cause them to become such outsiders.

## Love

Duffy does not present us with a romantic, fairy-tale view of love. In fact, from the poems in the *Anthology*, it could be argued that Duffy has a cynical attitude to love. 'Anne Hathaway' is a beautiful sonnet expressing Anne's love for her husband — but he is now dead and all she has left to remember him is 'the bed [they] loved in'. 'Havisham' contains the vitriolic words of a woman destroyed when her 'Beloved sweetheart bastard' abandoned her. 'Salome' shows a heroine who had no love for the countless men she slept with.

There is genuine love shown between Duffy and her mother in 'Before You Were Mine' as they danced home from Mass, 'stamping stars'. Elvis's twin has enthusiasm and love of life: 'Lawdy./I'm alive and well'. We could see this as a love of Christ, as may be expected from a nun — even if this is not made obvious.

## Outsiders

The key thing about the characters featured in 'Education for Leisure' and 'Stealing' is that they appear to be loveless. We could assume that they have never loved or been loved, and that it is this that makes them so destructive. The narrator in

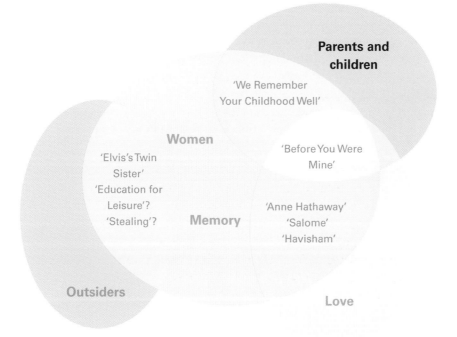

Figure 2 Duffy's themes

the former poem may, narcissistically, love himself (he calls himself a 'genius' and a 'superstar'), but he has no love for anything else, which makes him capable of squashing flies, harming his pets and committing cold-blooded murder. Similarly, the thief in 'Stealing' takes a snowman so he has a 'mate' (presumably because he has no human friends), and then goes on to enjoy the fact that 'children would cry in the morning'.

Other outsiders might include Miss Havisham, who cut herself off from the world on the day that she was jilted at the altar. As a result her mind and spirit ended up broken: 'Don't think it's only the heart that b-b-b-breaks' ('Havisham'). Perhaps Salome too was a social outsider and realised that she needed 'to clean up [her] act' to become an accepted member of society ('Salome').

However, Duffy also hints that being an outsider is not necessarily a bad thing. Elvis's twin cut herself off from the world outside the convent when she became a nun, and sees it as a better life: 'I think of it/as Graceland here,/a land of grace' ('Elvis's Twin Sister').

# Armitage

## Family relationships

Some of the poems in this *Anthology* are about Armitage's own family and his experiences, some may be about other families Armitage has known. Crucially, they could be about any family and anyone's experiences in that family. As a poet, Armitage is sharing his impressions of life, and we are invited to think about our own family experiences in this light.

He recounts ordinary happenings that must take place every day in homes around the country. 'Homecoming' is about an unidentified family with a teenage child, and an argument that blows up when the teenager's yellow jacket gets dirty at school. In poems that both subtly express his love for his parents and assert his independence from them, he recalls his father's attitude to his (Armitage's) newly pierced ear ('My father thought it bloody queer') and describes setting up his own home for the first time with this mother's help ('Mother, any distance greater'). 'November' centres on the grandmother of a friend of Armitage's as she approaches the end of her life and is taken to a care home ('We have brought her here to die').

It could be said that Armitage's work, like Shakespeare's Seven Ages of Man speech in *As You Like It* (Act 2, Scene 7), shows the entire lifespan of a person. Shakespeare describes the 'infant, schoolboy, lover, soldier, justice, slipper'd pantaloon and second childishness'. Armitage presents us with five stages: the school pupil and then lover ('Homecoming'); someone leaving home for the first time ('Mother, any distance greater'); a disaffected employee ('Hitcher': *One more sick-note, mister, and you're finished. Fired*'); and old women at the end of their lives, with 'pasty bloodless smiles' and 'stunned brains' ('November').

## Gaining independence

Freedom is very important to Armitage and is a theme that he explores in a number of these poems. However, we are left to ask: how complete is the independence achieved, and at what cost? In 'Mother, any distance greater' the extended metaphor of the tape measure being unwound comes to a climax when Armitage gets to the 'loft' and doesn't know whether he will 'fall or fly' when he lets go. Independence is not gained by the teenager in 'Homecoming' until over 'sixteen years' later, when a lover's embrace brings release from the tensions caused by the argument over the yellow jacket. The friend's grandmother finally loses her independence in 'November': 'It is time John.'

Independence is also an issue in two poems where Armitage takes on a persona. In 'Those bastards in their mansions' the narrator enjoys the freedom to 'stick to the shadows' and 'carry a gun', away from the 'cuffs and shackles' weighing down the other people dependent on the 'lords and ladies'. In a different way, the man who picks up a hitchhiker struggles between independence and dependence ('Hitcher'). Although he does not care about his job, he appears locked into consumerism (he shows off about his 'ansaphone' and 'hired' car). He is therefore violently jealous of the truly independent hippie to whom he gives a lift, who 'was following the sun to west from east/with just a toothbrush'.

However, in 'Kid' independence is celebrated. Robin, finally free of Batman's bossy 'big shot' influence, is free to live a normal life and has come out 'taller, harder, stronger, older'.

## Attitudes to death

The character in 'Hitcher' who hits his passenger six times 'in the face' with a 'krooklok' and then pushes him out of the car seems unaffected by death. We are not told whether the hitchhiker lives or dies — the driver does not care. It is also suggested that the gun-carrying character in 'Those bastards in their mansions' would not be afraid to use it if necessary.

These attitudes do not reflect Armitage's own views, of course. He has clearly thought about death a lot: there is a whole sonnet on what will happen to his body after his death, 'I've made out a will'. More poignant is 'November', where, having seen the physical and mental decay of the old women in the care home, Armitage and his friend 'feel the terror' of approaching death and know they are powerless to do anything about it: 'we let it happen. We can say nothing.' In this poem, life seems reduced to one long approach to death, with only occasional brighter moments: 'Sometimes the sun spangles and we feel alive.'

## Love

The fact that Armitage wishes his heart alone, 'the pendulum, the ticker', not to be donated to the National Health Service is interesting ('I've made out a will'). Perhaps it is the association between the heart and love that makes him wish to retain it (although he does not specify what will happen to it).

There are different kinds of love featured in these poems. Romantic love appears in 'Homecoming', where a trusted lover's act of folding their loved one into their arms heals the pain of over 16 years. (This is in contrast to the sordid affair Batman conducted with the married woman in 'Kid': 'Holy robin-redbreast-nest-egg-shocker!') The mutual love of parents and children is shown in 'My father thought it bloody queer', where Armitage is moved to remember his father's exact words a long time afterwards, and again in 'Mother, any distance greater', where his mother's 'fingertips still pinch/the last one-hundredth of an inch' of the tape measure and she is his 'Anchor'.

The callous driver in 'Hitcher' and, perhaps, the shadowy figure in 'Those bastards in their mansions' are characterised by their inability to feel love. This suggests that it is their lovelessness that enables them to act as they do.

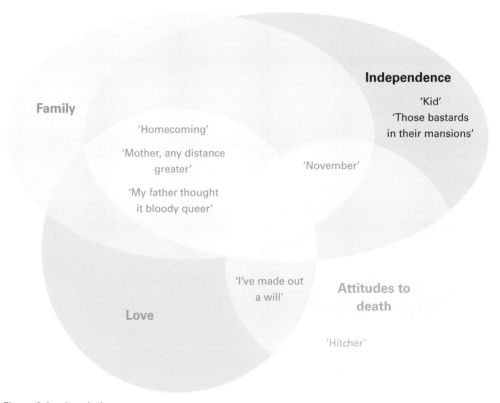

Figure 3 Armitage's themes

# Themes shared by Duffy and Armitage

Duffy and Armitage explore some similar ideas through their poetry.

## Love

Duffy and Armitage focus on different kinds of love in different ways. For example, Duffy's 'Anne Hathaway' describes romantic love very sensuously: 'Romance/and drama played by touch, by scent, by taste'. The disappointed lover in 'Havisham' may hate the man who jilted her by day, but dreams of making love to him at night: 'the lost body over me,/my fluent tongue in its mouth in its ear'. Armitage is more restrained, using the metaphor of putting on the yellow cotton jacket to describe a lovers' embrace – 'These ribs are pleats or seams. These arms are sleeves' ('Homecoming').

> ### Key point
>
> Both Armitage and Duffy write sometimes from an intensely **personal** point of view: each writes about their *own* thoughts, memories, emotions and reactions. At other times, they take on a **persona** and write from the point of view of somebody else, which allows them to explore the motivations, thoughts and feelings of others. Almost all the poems by Armitage and Duffy in the *Anthology* are written in the first person.

## The family, or parents and children

One type of love is that within a family. Duffy shows the love she feels for her mother in 'Before You Were Mine' through the vivid and affectionate portrayal of the young woman who would 'sparkle and waltz and laugh'. Similarly understated is the love Armitage has for both his mother and his father. His mother provides safety, a refuge: 'Anchor' ('Mother, any distance greater') and his father's words live on in his memory ('My father thought it bloody queer').

This contrasts with the bitterness felt between the parents and child of Duffy's 'We Remember Your Childhood Well' — there is a disturbing vindictiveness in the parents' words, 'No, no, nobody left the skidmarks of sin/on your soul and laid you wide open for Hell'. Armitage shows the breakdown of a close relationship in 'Kid'. Batman had reputedly been 'like an elder brother' or 'like a father' to Robin, but Robin scornfully overturns these ideas and celebrates his independence: 'I'm not playing ball boy any longer'. Both poets, therefore, show the range of emotions that can be felt within a family.

## Death

Although it is not such a major theme in her poetry as in Armitage's, Duffy is interested in death and our attitude to death. 'Anne Hathaway' is about a woman who has lost her husband, although the death is not directly mentioned. Without

the subtitle about Shakespeare's will, the only hard evidence to indicate to the reader that Anne's lover has died is reserved until the penultimate line: 'I hold him in the casket of my <u>widow</u>'s head'. This is the only phrase in the present tense in the whole poem: Anne seems to live in the past, in the life before death.

Salome seems almost unconcerned about the decapitation of a man in her bed. We are not sure whether her exclamation, 'ain't life a bitch', indicates sympathy for John the Baptist or is a comment on her own situation. The character in 'Education for Leisure' is even less concerned, appearing to be stimulated by the idea of going out to commit murder: the persona notes that 'The pavements glitter suddenly', as if something important is about to happen. This is similar to the driver in 'Hitcher', who casually pushes the hitchhiker he has just beaten out of the car without knowing whether he is dead or alive — and not caring: 'Stitch that, I remember thinking'.

Generally, however, Armitage presents a more reflective attitude to death, particularly in 'November'. The sight of old women approaching death fills him and his friend with 'terror' and a hopelessness about their own lives: 'we watch the evening, failing again'. There is a hint that Armitage's father has died in 'My father thought it bloody queer'. His father's words move him and his 'own voice break[s] like a tear'. Both these examples indicate a more personal exploration of death than that in Duffy's poems.

## Conflict

Both poets touch on the theme of conflict in the set poems. Miss Havisham's fight is with her ex-fiancé and is shown through her violent actions — 'I stabbed at a wedding-cake' ('Havisham'). The conflict between the parents and child in 'We Remember Your Childhood Well' is only hinted at — 'Nobody turned off the light and argued/with somebody else all night.' However, the conflict in 'Salome' and 'Education for Leisure' is more brutal (as explained above).

Similarly, Armitage explores a range of conflicts, from the gentle conflict between himself and his father over the pierced ear ('My father thought it bloody queer'), through the rows in 'Homecoming' and 'Kid' that led to people distancing themselves from each other, to potential murders in 'Those bastards in their mansions' and 'Hitcher'.

### Review your learning

Quick questions (answers are given on page 100):

1 What are the main themes in Duffy's poetry?

2 What are the main themes in Armitage's poetry?

3 Which of the following themes does Duffy *not* write about?

childhood      death      love      nature      the family

**4** Which of the following themes does Armitage *not* write about?

death        his family        war        independence        love

Longer questions:

**5** Complete Table 1 to show some poems on various themes that you might want to compare. Use any poems which are appropriate: you will find that there are a number of poems that could fill each box.

Table 1 Themes in Duffy and Armitage

**6**

|  | Duffy | Armitage |
|---|---|---|
| Family; parents and children |  |  |
| Love |  |  |
| Death |  |  |
| Conflict |  |  |

Briefly sum up each poet's attitude to the themes they share.

# Style

As you read this section, ask yourself:
- ➤ Why is it important to recognise a poem's viewpoint?
- ➤ What do the setting and atmosphere contribute to a poem?
- ➤ How do symbolism and imagery affect a poem?
- ➤ How have the poets used rhythm, rhyme and metre?

As well as considering *what* a poet writes about, it is important to consider *how* they write. In good poetry, the way in which ideas are expressed helps to convey the message or to emphasise what is being said. This section looks at the styles adopted by Duffy and Armitage and a number of the poets in the Pre-1914 Poetry Bank, pointing out key aspects. Of course, it is often hard to look at each aspect in isolation because the language is so dense that techniques overlap each other, but it is important to recognise the main ones.

Table 2 on pages 78–79 summarises the poetic techniques used in all the poems discussed in the guide.

**Key point**

Check the 'Glossary of literary terms' at the end of the book if you need to remind yourself about any of the features mentioned in this section.

## Viewpoint

Almost all of the poems by Duffy and Armitage in your *Anthology* are written in the **first person**. (The exceptions are Duffy's 'We Remember Your Childhood Well' and Armitage's 'Homecoming', both of which are written in the **second person**.) Armitage's autobiographical poems are intensely personal and so convey his own thoughts and feelings. Through telling us about everyday events, he reveals to us things that are intimate and obviously important to him. For example, in 'My Father thought it bloody queer' Armitage describes his father's reaction when he has his ear pierced. The memory of his father's words, years later, 'cried from way back in the spiral of the ear', as if it was coming from the very core of his thoughts. Although he may not have registered it at the time, Armitage now recognises that his father's words were precious.

In this collection, Duffy's most personal poem is 'Before You Were Mine'. The young Duffy herself does not feature very much, as the focus is on her mother ten years before Duffy was born ('I'm not here yet'), so there is less intimacy than in some of Armitage's work.

Some of the pre-1914 poems also use the **first person** and, again, we are witness to the poets' innermost thoughts. For example:

* Jonson writes movingly about his emotions in 'On my first Sonne' and we see the tension he feels between mourning his beloved child, 'his best piece of poetrie', and convincing himself that the boy is in a better place with God.
* Tichborne in his 'Elegy' mourns his own imminent death in a surprisingly calm, controlled, lucid manner: 'My glass is full, and now my glass is run;/And now I live, and now my life is done.'
* Clare writes frankly about the joy a beautiful landscape can give. His 'Sonnet' is an outpouring of gratitude for a sunny summer's day.

In most of Duffy's poems and half of Armitage's, the thoughts of a real or fictional character are presented: the poets have each adopted a **persona**. The style in which they write reflects the character they are presenting. For instance:

* Duffy gives Miss Havisham language full of bitterness and pent-up violence ('I could strangle [him]', 'Puce curses', 'I stabbed at a wedding-cake') to show how desperate and mad she has become ('Havisham'). In contrast, Elvis's twin uses relaxed slang ('Lawdy./I'm alive and well') to show how content she is in her convent ('Elvis's Twin Sister').
* Armitage gives Robin lots of slang expressions like 'big shot' and 'blown the cover' to show his youth and his new-found confidence now that he is independent of Batman ('Kid'). The driver in 'Hitcher' uses clichés like 'under the weather' to indicate his lack of imagination.

It is also true that the pre-1914 poets write in a style that reflects the characters they adopt:

* Wordsworth takes on the persona of a woman who is wild with worry because she has lost contact with her only son, in 'The Affliction of Margaret'. She asks: 'Was darkness ever like to this?' The long, detailed poem suggests the length of time she has spent grieving and wondering over his absence.
* In 'The Laboratory' by Browning (another example of a male poet adopting a female persona) we see a woman bent on vengeance, fascinated by the method the alchemist in her pay is using to murder her rival.

> **Key point**
>
> Another name for colloquial speech, including slang, is the **vernacular**. You could say, for example, 'Duffy's presentation of Salome includes phrases in the vernacular, such as "the booze and the fags and the sex", to help us picture her as a casual and immoral woman'.

* Hardy becomes a jobbing soldier in 'The Man He Killed' and we see a simple man grappling to make sense of war. He uses dialect and slang appropriate to the character.

Two poems in the selection, Blake's 'The Little Boy Lost/Found' and Tennyson's 'The Eagle', are written in the **third person**, from the perspective of an omniscient (all-knowing) narrator. The poets act as reporters or storytellers, relaying to us what happens. At the same time, what they tell us is carefully chosen to contribute to the subject, atmosphere and tone of what they are writing about.

# Setting and atmosphere

Duffy and Armitage both convey a sense of place in their poetry. This is not merely to set the scene for us, but to create atmosphere too. For example:

* Duffy lets us hear the Gregorian chant that Elvis's twin hears in her convent, ('*Pascha nostrum immolatus est*') to create a strong sense of place and suggest the comforting beauty of the music ('Elvis's Twin Sister'). In contrast, in 'Before You Were Mine' she conjures up the glamorous excitement of a Glasgow 'ballroom with the thousand eyes' so that we can feel the thrill her mother once experienced.
* Armitage concentrates on creating more down-to-earth settings. He suggests the daunting nature of the task of decorating his new home when he talks of 'the acres of the walls, the prairies of the floors' ('Mother, any distance greater'). The stark nature of the old people's care home in 'November' is conveyed through the bleak description of the 'rough blankets' and the fact that the grandmother 'sinks down into her incontinence' — we had expected to read that she was sinking down into a comfortable bed.

Creating a setting which produces atmosphere was also important for the pre-1914 poets:

* Whitman begins 'Patrolling Barnegat' with 'Wild, wild the storm', the repetition suggesting the strength of the weather.
* Tennyson seems to be pointing out the backdrop for us: 'There lies the port; the vessel puffs her sail:/There gloom the dark broad seas.' The use of 'gloom' hints that the enthusiastic sailors will have challenges to face and so creates tension in the poem.

# Symbolism

Symbols are used by poets rather like pictures in a book — to illustrate a point more clearly, or to leave a vivid impression of an idea. A **symbol** is one thing that represents another thing or idea: it can be the central theme of a poem, or can develop a particular idea within a poem. Duffy, Armitage and the pre-1914 poets sometimes use symbols to enrich or clarify their work:

* Duffy uses the bed that Shakespeare left his wife in his will as inspiration for 'Anne Hathaway': the bed in which they had loved becomes a symbol of their love.
* The 'canary-yellow cotton jacket' that features in Armitage's 'Homecoming' symbolises the teenager's relationship with her family. When the jacket becomes dirty on 'a cloakroom floor', the relationship with her parents is also spoiled. It is only when a lover can enfold her in his arms many years later, as if he was enfolding her in the jacket, that she feels at home again.
* The child in Blake's 'The Little Boy Lost/Found' could be a symbol for all human beings. Blake is suggesting that we can all wander away into danger and we all need God to bring us back to safety.
* The burn that Hopkins describes in 'Inversnaid' is a symbol of all the water in the world. By showing how the stream is important to the Highland landscape, Hopkins is able to put over his wider point about preserving the 'wet and…wildness'.

# Imagery

Imagery, like symbolism, is a way for poets to add word pictures to their poems. Imagery includes figures of speech such as **similes**, **metaphors** and **personification** to illustrate ideas. These are often most successful when they are tied in with the poet's **themes** (look back at the 'Themes' section for more ideas).

Duffy's startling use of metaphor in 'Havisham' is a good illustration. She presents us with Miss Havisham's hard, cold eyes that are 'dark green pebbles' and veins on the back of her hands that are 'ropes' she 'could strangle with'. The harsh images reflect the sour hostility that Miss Havisham feels towards her former lover. An entirely different mood is created in 'Anne Hathaway', when metaphor is piled on metaphor to suggest the utter escape that the bed represented to Shakespeare and his wife: 'The bed we loved in was a spinning world/of forests, castles, torchlight, clifftops, seas'.

Armitage also uses original and striking imagery. There is an effective extended metaphor in 'Mother, any distance greater' in which the relationship between mother and son spools out like a measuring tape. When Armitage was born he was 'at the zero-end'; the years 'unreel' until his mother clings on to 'the last one-hundredth of an inch' and finally 'breaking point' is reached. There are further metaphors in 'I've made out a will', where Armitage wryly reduces the parts of his body to the stock of an open-all-hours shop: 'jellies and tubes and syrups and glues'.

Table 2 Poetic techniques

| | First person | Persona | Second person | Vernacular | Iambic pentameter | Regular stanzas | Rhyme | Sonnet |
|---|---|---|---|---|---|---|---|---|
| **Duffy** | | | | | | | | |
| 'Havisham' | | ✓ | | ✓ | | ✓ | | |
| 'Elvis's Twin Sister' | | ✓ | | ✓ | | ✓ | ✓ | |
| 'Anne Hathaway' | | ✓ | | | ✓ | | | ✓ |
| 'Salome' | | ✓ | | ✓ | | | ✓ | |
| 'Before You Were Mine' | ✓ | | (✓) | | | ✓ | | |
| 'We Remember Your Childhood Well' | | | ✓ | | | ✓ | ✓ | |
| 'Education for Leisure' | | ✓ | | ✓ | | ✓ | | |
| 'Stealing' | | ✓ | | ✓ | | ✓ | | |
| **Armitage** | | | | | | | | |
| 'Mother, any distance greater' | ✓ | | | | | | ✓ | |
| 'My father thought it bloody queer' | ✓ | | | ✓ | | | ✓ | |
| 'Homecoming' | | | ✓ | | | | | |
| 'November' | ✓ | | | | | ✓ | ✓ | |
| 'Kid' | | ✓ | | ✓ | ✓ | | ✓ | |
| 'Those bastards in their mansions' | | ✓ | | ✓ | | | ✓ | ✓ |
| 'I've made out a will' | ✓ | | | | ✓ | | (✓) | ✓ |
| 'Hitcher' | | ✓ | | ✓ | | ✓ | (✓) | |

| | First person | Persona | Second person | Vernacular | Iambic pentameter | Regular stanzas | Rhyme | Sonnet |
|---|---|---|---|---|---|---|---|---|
| **Pre-1914 Poetry Bank** | | | | | | | | |
| 'On my first Sonne' | ✓ | | | | | | ✓ | |
| 'The Song of the Old Mother' | | ✓ | | | | | ✓ | |
| 'The Affliction of Margaret' | | ✓ | | | | ✓ | ✓ | |
| 'The Little Boy Lost/ Found' | | | | | | ✓ | ✓ | |
| 'Tichborne's Elegy' | ✓ | | | | | ✓ | ✓ | |
| 'The Man He Killed' | | ✓ | | ✓ | | ✓ | ✓ | |
| 'Patrolling Barnegat' | ✓ | | | | | | ✓ | |
| 'Sonnet 130' | (✓) | | | | | | ✓ | ✓ |
| 'My Last Duchess' | | ✓ | | | ✓ | | ✓ | |
| 'The Laboratory' | | ✓ | | | | ✓ | ✓ | |
| 'Ulysses' | | ✓ | | | ✓ | | | |
| 'The Village Schoolmaster' | | ✓ | | | ✓ | | ✓ | |
| 'The Eagle' | | | | | | ✓ | ✓ | |
| 'Inversnaid' | ✓ | | | | | ✓ | ✓ | |
| 'Sonnet' | ✓ | | | | ✓ | | ✓ | ✓ |

'Tichborne's Elegy' consists almost entirely of metaphors, as it illustrates how his life is being cut short: 'My prime of youth is but a frost of cares,/My feast of joy is but a dish of pain'. Here imagery emphasises tragedy. Shakespeare plays with similes in a near-comic way throughout 'Sonnet 130', pretending to try to find images that describe his lover honestly and without using clichés: 'My mistress' eyes are nothing like the sun'.

## Alliteration and assonance

Where imagery could be said to add pictures to a poem, **alliteration** and **assonance** add the sound effects. Sometimes these techniques bind ideas together. Examples include Duffy's 'Anne Hathaway' in which Shakespeare is described as 'My living laughing love', and Armitage describing his skeleton as 'the chassis or cage or cathedral of bone' ('I've made out a will').

Alliteration works most effectively when the sound of the words echoes the sense. The 'red balloon bursting' at the end of Duffy's 'Havisham' prepares us for the final words of the poem, 'Don't think it's only the heart that b-b-b-breaks'. The repeated letter 'b' sounds like someone breaking down and sobbing, which is exactly what we can imagine Miss Havisham does.

Of the pre-1914 poets, Whitman and Hopkins perhaps use these sound effects most effectively. The intensity of the 's' sounds in 'On beachy slush and sand spirts of snow fierce slanting' (where alliteration combines with **consonance**) enables us to hear the snow shooting down the beach, and Whitman describes the throaty 'hoarse roar' of the waves ('Patrolling Barnegat'). Hopkins combines alliteration and assonance in one rushing line, 'His rollrock highroad roaring down', to give an impression of the turbulent, dancing water ('Inversnaid').

## Rhythm, rhyme and metre

Duffy chooses a variety of forms in which to write her poems, all of them suitable for the subject. While 'Anne Hathaway' is a sonnet consisting of regular **iambic pentameters**, echoing the sonnets that Shakespeare himself wrote, 'Elvis's Twin Sister' uses short lines reminiscent of Elvis's song lyrics. Most of the featured poems have regular stanzas, but 'Salome' is more loosely structured, perhaps in keeping with the loose morals of its subject.

Often Duffy chooses not to end-stop the lines but uses **enjambement** so that the sense flows on between the lines, adding to the conversational style. This is chilling in 'Stealing', where we can hear the punctuated speech of the thief ('I wanted him, a mate/with a mind as cold as the slice of ice'); the line break in 'my breath ripped out/in rags' dramatises the sense. She sometimes uses **rhyme** to create effects. The irregular '-ter' rhymes in 'Salome' suggest impatience or the slurring of someone who has had too much to drink; the irregular rhymes in 'We Remember Your Childhood Well' perhaps suggest the irregularity in the child's life.

Armitage uses **rhyme** in a similar sort of way. 'Kid' perhaps provides the wittiest example of rhyme, where the constant '-er' rhymes recall the Batman theme tune, in contrast to 'My father thought it bloody queer', where heavy irregular rhymes such as 'head'/'led'/'instead' echo the downbeat mood of the poem.

Armitage often writes in **regular stanzas**, sometimes altering the form slightly for effect. For example, in 'November', which is based on three-line stanzas, a line is 'missing' from the final stanza, so that the poem concludes on a couplet. Perhaps this suggests a cutting short of life. 'Hitcher' consists of five equal stanzas, but the line lengths within each stanza vary markedly, perhaps to indicate the instability of the driver.

Because of the time in which they were written, most of the pre-1914 poems have a tight structure. Stanzas, where used, are of equal length and may chart the progression of a narrative, each stanza dealing with an addition to the 'story' (as in 'The Affliction of Margaret', 'The Man He Killed' and 'The Laboratory'). Many of the poems have a fixed **rhyme scheme**. Sometimes the rhyme scheme is disguised, as in 'My Last Duchess', where the use of enjambement means that the rhyming couplets are not immediately obvious (and so the Duke's words appear more natural). In other poems the rhyme scheme is brought to the fore and is used to emphasise the meaning of the poem. For example, 'The Song of the Old Mother' concludes with 'old' rhyming with 'cold', heavy words to reflect the woman's heaviness of heart. The later poems, such as Whitman's 'Patrolling Barnegat', are less formally structured. Here the lines are much longer than usual and all lines end with an identical musical yet menacing '-ing' rhyme.

# The poets' choice of language

It goes almost without saying that poets choose their style of language carefully to fit their subject matter. Both Duffy and Armitage frequently use the **vernacular** when that would be the language used by the characters they are presenting. This includes dialect as well as slang. Duffy shows us how Elvis's sister speaks in an American drawl, 'y'all' ('Elvis's Twin Sister'), as does Armitage's Robin, 'you baby' ('Kid'). A sense of history is indicated by Armitage in 'Those bastards in their mansions' through the inclusion of details such as 'stocking feet and threadbare britches' and 'cuffs and shackles'.

In the pre-1914 selection, there is a great contrast between Tennyson's brief, stark, strictly rhyming fragment of 'The Eagle' and the richly detailed, flowing 'Ulysses'. Much of Hardy's poetry is detailed and romantic, yet in 'The Man He Killed' he deliberately uses simple, colloquial language suitable for the ordinary

soldier whose persona he adopts: 'We should have sat us down to wet/Right many a nipperkin!'

**Review your learning**

Quick questions: true or false? (Answers are given on page 100.)

1 Both Duffy and Armitage write in the third person.

2 A symbol is an object or image which represents another thing or idea.

3 'Spinster. I stink and remember' ('Havisham') is an example of alliteration.

4 'And as for the latter,/it was time to turf out the blighter/the beater or biter' ('Salome') is an example of assonance.

5 'Kid' is written in iambic pentameters.

Longer questions:

6 Choose a poem by Duffy that includes **rhyme**. Write a paragraph explaining what the rhyme contributes.

7 Choose a poem by Armitage that includes some striking **enjambement** and try to explain its effect. You could concentrate on two or three lines only.

8 Choose one poem by Duffy and one by Armitage that include the use of the **vernacular** (informal language and slang). How does the use of such language contribute to our understanding of the characters?

# Comparing poems

As you read this section, ask yourself:
➢ Which aspects should I concentrate on when comparing poems?
➢ What type of things should I look for?
➢ What are the best methods to use when comparing poems?

## A comparison of themes

Table 3 on pages 84–85 suggests some ways in which the themes of all the poems you have studied could be compared. It does not cover every single point that could be compared, but it does give you an idea of how to group various poems and begin to work out the similarities and differences between them.

You may wish to develop the table: copy it out and add extra columns, or add more detailed cross-references.

## How to compare poems

It can be daunting to be asked to compare poems, especially as each poem was written to be read on its own and not to be analysed in an examination. However, it is not too hard if you approach the poems with the right questions. You will be asked to compare four poems. For each one, ask yourself:

* What is the **subject matter**? What is the story of the poem? What is it about?
* Whose **viewpoint** do we see things from? Is it in the first, second or third person? If the first person, is it the poet talking or have they taken on a persona?
* What is the **main theme**, or is there more than one main theme? What are the main ideas that the poet wants to explore? Look at Table 3 on pages 84–85 to help you.

Table 3 Comparing themes

| | Looking back; memories | Family; parent/child | Love, relationships, friendship | Death | Conflict |
|---|---|---|---|---|---|
| **Duffy** | | | | | |
| 'Havisham' | ✓ | | ✓ | | ✓ |
| 'Elvis's Twin Sister' | ✓ | | ✓ | | |
| 'Anne Hathaway' | ✓ | | ✓ | ✓ | |
| 'Salome' | ✓ | | ✓ | ✓ | ✓ |
| 'Before You Were Mine' | ✓ | ✓ | ✓ | | |
| 'We Remember Your Childhood Well' | ✓ | ✓ | | | ✓ |
| 'Education for Leisure' | | | | ✓ | ✓ |
| 'Stealing' | ✓ | | | | (✓) |
| **Armitage** | | | | | |
| 'Mother, any distance greater' | ✓ | ✓ | | | |
| 'My father thought it bloody queer' | ✓ | ✓ | | | ✓ |
| 'Homecoming' | ✓ | ✓ | ✓ | | ✓ |
| 'November' | | ✓ | ✓ | ✓ | |
| 'Kid' | ✓ | (✓) | ✓ | | ✓ |
| 'Those bastards in their mansions' | | | | | ✓ |
| 'I've made out a will' | | | ✓ | ✓ | |
| 'Hitcher' | | | ✓ | ✓ | ✓ |

| | Looking back; memories | Family; parent/ child | Love, relationships, friendship | Death | Conflict |
|---|---|---|---|---|---|
| **Pre-1914 Poetry Bank** | | | | | |
| 'On my first Sonne' | | ✓ | | ✓ | |
| 'The Song of the Old Mother' | ✓ | | ✓ | | |
| 'The Affliction of Margaret' | ✓ | ✓ | | ✓ | |
| 'The Little Boy Lost/ Found' | | ✓ | ✓ | | |
| 'Tichborne's Elegy' | ✓ | | | | (✓) |
| 'The Man He Killed' | ✓ | | ✓ | ✓ | ✓ |
| 'Patrolling Barnegat' | | | | | ✓ |
| 'Sonnet 130' | | | ✓ | | |
| 'My Last Duchess' | ✓ | | ✓ | ✓ | ✓ |
| 'The Laboratory' | | | ✓ | ✓ | ✓ |
| 'Ulysses' | ✓ | ✓ | | ✓ | ✓ |
| 'The Village Schoolmaster' | ✓ | | ✓ | | |
| 'The Eagle' | | | | | ✓ |
| 'Inversnaid' | | | ✓ | | |
| 'Sonnet' | | | ✓ | | |

* How does the poet **convey their message**? What are the key **images** and/or the main **features** of the poem? What **techniques** does the poet use? Look back at the notes on 'Structure', 'Language' and 'Imagery' in this book.

* What is the **tone** or **mood**? Think about how the poem should be read aloud — perhaps joyfully? Mournfully? Fearfully? With admiration? Lovingly? Angrily? Look back at the notes on 'Ideas to consider' in this book.

* What is your **own response**? Do you like the poem? Try to give a reason for your answer. What does it make you think of? What strikes you most about it? Look back at the 'Ideas to consider' in this book.

Perhaps the easiest way to approach comparative questions is to begin by making a table — then you can see if you have missed anything out. Let's say you want to look at four poems to **explore the relationship between parents and children**. You might choose 'Before You Were Mine', 'Homecoming', 'On my first Sonne' and 'The Little Boy Lost/Found'.

You could begin by producing something like Table 4. Of course, this could be extended for other poems that include the relationships between parents and children, or you could make similar tables for the other themes.

Alternatively, you could make structured notes on each poem in turn. If, for example, you are asked to **explore the poets' presentation of memory** in four poems, you might select 'My father thought it bloody queer', 'Havisham', 'The Man He Killed', and 'Ulysses', and jot down ideas like this:

'My father thought it bloody queer': memory vividly reconstructed, word for word. First person — autobiographical? We're presented with two memories — the ear being pierced and the father's reaction; the exact words come back to the poet years later. Vernacular adds immediacy.

'Havisham': her memories are detailed, bitter and vengeful. Poet takes on the persona of a gnarled old woman who has violent thoughts towards the man who jilted her ('Not a day since I haven't wished him dead'), yet memory hasn't dulled the passion she still feels ('my fluent tongue in its mouth in its ear').

'The Man He Killed': memories brief yet reflective. Poet takes on a persona — use of vernacular to suggest he was an ordinary soldier. Memories simple, not elaborated upon – 'I shot him dead'. Sense of confusion — soldier remembers the enemy as being just like him — he tries to rationalise war.

'Ulysses': sweeping memories of previous glory. Large scale — no details given; sense that he has many memories. Memories inspire him and motivate him: 'though/We are not now that strength which in old days/Moved earth and heaven; that which we are, we are'.

Table 4 Comparing poems

| | 'Before You Were Mine' | 'Homecoming' | 'On My First Sonne' | 'The Little Boy Lost/Found' |
|---|---|---|---|---|
| Subject matter | Duffy imagines her mother's exciting life before she was born | A teenager rows with their parents over a trivial incident — the wounds are not healed for years | Jonson mourns the death of his seven-year-old son | A young boy loses his father but is found by his mother — with the help of God |
| Viewpoint | Duffy's, looking back on her own childhood, then further back to her mother's youth | The lover's, who retells the story in the second person | Jonson's — a grieving parent | An omniscient observer (one who sees everything) |
| Theme(s) | Memories, parents and children | Parents and children; conflict; looking back | Parents and children; death | Parents and children; relationships; (and nature, as it is set in a 'mire' and a 'lonely' fen) |
| Style: structure, language and imagery | Regular stanzas with vivid imagery to express the 'brightness' of her mother's life | Four unequal stanzas, dealing with each stage of the narrative; yellow jacket is a symbol | Banking imagery: Jonson pays back God what is owed. Rhyming couplets | Sounds like a nursery rhyme — simple structure. God's role is unclear — sense of mystery |
| Ideas to consider: tone/mood | Affectionate but wistful? (The best times in her life were before Duffy was born) | We're invited to compare the love of a family (which cracks) with romantic love (which heals) | Heartfelt yet restrained | Sad and mournful when the child is lost; relieved and joyful when he's found |
| Ideas to consider: your response | Beautiful picture of fun times in the 1950s | Striking opening description of a trust exercise sets the tone for the poem | Brave: Jonson tries to persuade himself his son is now better off | Puzzling. What is significance of the 'vapour' and 'wand'ring light'? |

When you have jotted down notes, practise writing a few paragraphs outlining the comparisons you wish to make. Here are two paragraphs comparing four poems on the **theme of conflict**. The poems chosen were 'The Eagle', 'Hitcher', 'My Last Duchess', and 'Salome'.

Tennyson and Armitage both describe a single moment of conflict in precise detail. Tennyson seems to admire the majestic bird which swoops on its unwary

victim 'like a thunderbolt', while Armitage's bald presentation of the driver — 'I let him have it', 'Stitch that, I remember thinking' — shows his dislike of the character and disapproval of his actions. Tennyson is a spectator or reporter on the violence, while Armitage takes on a persona to enact it and make it vivid to the reader.

Browning and Duffy also present conflict from the perspective of a persona. Browning's Duke of Ferrara admits to being in conflict with his wife over her behaviour towards other men ('She had/A heart – how shall I say? – too soon made glad') and he hints that he took action to prevent it: 'I gave commands;/Then all smiles stopped together.' He does not appear to feel guilty for ending the conflict between them in the most violent way possible. Duffy, too, takes on a persona who seems to deny her guilt. It is not clear for whom we should feel sympathy when Salome realises the severed head of John the Baptist is in her bed: 'ain't life a bitch'. She hardly seems aware of the conflict between John and her mother, who had prompted her to ask for his death, as this is not mentioned in the poem.

It would be useful to practise writing similar paragraphs using four poems linked by other themes. The more connections and links between the poems you record, the easier it will be to choose poems that suit the question posed in the exam.

Remember, however, that not all questions in the exam will necessarily be theme-based. You may also be asked to look at four poems written in the first person, or four poems that use rhyme effectively. These paragraphs are about four **sonnets**: Clare's 'Sonnet', 'Sonnet 130', 'Anne Hathaway' and 'I've made out a will'.

Each of these sonnets has the theme of love, which is appropriate to the sonnet form. 'Anne Hathaway' is a beautiful poem in which Duffy takes on Anne's voice and remembers making love to Shakespeare. It is full of sensuous metaphor and word play, as in 'my body now a softer rhyme/to his'. It is interesting to compare this to Shakespeare's own love poem, 'Sonnet 130', which is more formal — but just as original. It turns on their head the clichéd statements that are often used in love poetry so that it can express genuine love for his mistress: 'I think my love as rare/As any she belied with false compare.'

Armitage's poem is more subtle. The love theme is not apparent until the final couplet, when he says he refuses to donate his heart to the National Health Service, despite the fact that he has willed away the rest of his body to the NHS. We assume that this is because the heart is associated with love, but there is no direct reference to this in the poem.

A less introspective poem, Clare's 'Sonnet' is a simple expression of personal joy at a beautiful view. He repeats 'I love to see', emphasising the pleasure he gains from looking at a peaceful, natural scene. He takes time to point out even the smallest elements — 'bright beetles in the clear lake play' — that participate in the 'beaming' summer's day.

You could use Table 2 on pages 78–79, which summarises poetic techniques, to practise linking other poems in this way.

There are also some sample exam questions in the section on 'Tackling the exam' (pages 94–96) that you can use to practise with.

# Tackling the exam

As you read this section, ask yourself:
- ➢ What grade are you aiming for?
- ➢ Which exam skills do you need to practise?
- ➢ How can you be sure you do what's needed on the day to gain your target grade?

The poetry question is worth a full **40%** of your entire English literature grade, so it is important to write the best answer you can to impress the examiners.

Let's remind ourselves of the **Assessment Objectives** (AO) for the English literature examination — in other words, what the examiners are looking for and what they are able to give marks for. Candidates are asked to:

* AO1: respond to texts critically, sensitively and in detail, selecting appropriate ways to convey their response, using textual evidence as appropriate.

* AO2: explore how language, structure and forms contribute to the meanings of texts, considering different approaches to texts and alternative interpretations.

* AO3: explore relationships and comparisons between texts, selecting and evaluating relevant material.

**Key point**

The Assessment Objectives are *equally weighted,* so you have to respond to each one to get a good grade. You are advised to spend roughly the same amount of time preparing for each Assessment Objective to be tested. In the past, some able candidates have let themselves down by ignoring one of the Assessment Objectives. However good your writing, you will not earn top marks if you don't discuss the poets' methods or you don't compare the poems!

# Examination tips: how to get a top mark

## Timing

Remember that you have just 1 hour and 45 minutes to complete both parts of the written paper. The exam board suggests you spend 45 minutes on Section A (prose text) and **1 hour on the poetry question**. You might want to do the poetry section first, when you are fresher, but do remember to allow yourself long enough for the prose question too: writing a fantastic answer on poetry but nothing on prose will lose you valuable marks.

Plan your hour carefully. You should spend:

* 5 minutes choosing which question to answer
* 10 minutes planning your answer
* 40 minutes writing
* 5 minutes checking your work.

## Read the questions carefully

The examiners try to set a range of questions that allow you to write about whatever poems you feel comfortable with, so read all the questions carefully to ensure that you spend your hour answering the question that is right for you. (Don't leap into the first question on the paper, or a question that happens to feature your favourite poem without considering how you would link it to three other poems.) When you have decided, write the number of the question in the box on the front of your answer paper, so that the examiner knows immediately what to expect.

## Planning your answer

* Use a highlighter pen to highlight key words or phrases in the poems so that you know what you are focusing on. As you are planning and writing, refer back frequently to make sure that you are actually answering the question.
* There is *no* requirement for balance. In other words, you do not have to write exactly the same amount on each of the four poems. However, you do need to show a good knowledge of each poem, so it is best to write more or less *similar* amounts on each one. (Writing four pages on two poems and only half a page on the other two is unlikely to show your full appreciation of the poems' meanings and ideas.)
* Remember that if a question is presented in two parts, it is important to devote equal weight to both parts. You can, if you wish, write a two-part essay for a two-part question (unless the wording of the question makes clear that you should write an integrated essay).
* For each poem, try to comment on each of the aspects discussed earlier in this book (see Table 4 on page 87). You need to consider what the poets wanted to say and how they said it, so jot down the main points on:
  * subject matter

* viewpoint
* themes
* structure, language and imagery
* ideas to consider — mood or tone
* ideas to consider — your response

Then work out how you will include these points in your essay.

## Choosing your language

You will impress the examiner by the elegance of your writing and the way in which you present your ideas. Guide the reader through your writing with phrases like those below. All of the following examples could come from an essay comparing the attitudes of the Duke of Ferrara ('My Last Duchess', Browning) and Ulysses ('Ulysses', Tennyson) towards other people. You can vary the phrases to suit any essay you are writing. Key phrases are in italic and those particular to the examples being discussed are in normal type.

### Introductory phrases

* *Perhaps the most striking thing about these poems* is that both men are clearly powerful rulers, *yet both poets allow us to explore* why it is that the Duke and Ulysses act as they do.
* *One theme that unites these poems is* reflection: both men look back to events in the past.
* *It may be because these poems were written* only three *years apart that* they share many ideas and themes.
* *On first reading, the two poems seem very similar because* both feature powerful men who have control over life and death. *However*, it becomes apparent that the Duke wields this power for selfish reasons, while Ulysses is arguably less selfish, hoping to do 'Some work of noble note'.
* *When I first read* 'Ulysses' *I was puzzled that* the hero could leave his country with his son in charge, *but* when I read 'My Last Duchess' I realised that this is preferable to being ruled over by a tyrant.

### Comparing similar features

* *Both poems are written* in the first person: Browning and Tennyson bring the characters to life by taking on their personas.
* *The effective use of* the iambic pentameter in 'Ulysses' *also features in* 'My Last Duchess', to give the impression of the patterns of natural speech.
* 'Ulysses' *includes an idea also contained in* 'My Last Duchess': neither the Duke nor Ulysses is attached to their wives.
* *Like* 'My Last Duchess', 'Ulysses' ends on an intriguing note: we don't know whether the Duke will obtain his 'fair' new wife or whether Ulysses' mission 'to seek, to find' will succeed.

* *I feel the two poems are alike because* of the strong image that is portrayed not only of both men but of their motives.

**Contrasting different features**

* *While* the Duke *refers to* the recent past, Ulysses concentrates on his memories of further back — the great successes of his youth.
* *However*, Ulysses' friendly relationship with his servants *is different to* the Duke's commanding attitude.
* *Unlike* 'Ulysses', *which is written in* blank verse, 'My Last Duchess' is composed of rhyming couplets — although they are not immediately obvious as they are not all end-stopped.
* *I feel the two poems are different because of* the scale of their subjects. 'My Last Duchess' is, arguably, little more than the tale of a jealous husband, while 'Ulysses' takes on a grander perspective.
* *The main contrast between* 'Ulysses' *and* 'My Last Duchess' *is* that Ulysses is a sympathetic hero (whom we can admire even if we do not agree with his actions), *while* the Duke is certainly a villain.
* *Although it could be said* that we learn more about the other characters in 'My Last Duchess' (including the duchess herself and Frà Pandolf), *I think that* Ulysses' praise of his son Telemachus is important.

**Concluding phrases**

* *In conclusion, both poems* provide a dramatic illustration of how powerful men may treat other people.
* *Having explored the poems carefully, it seems that* both the Duke and Ulysses are well practised in dealing with other people. Both have found ways of treating their family and servants to achieve their own goals.
* *What I will remember about these poems is* the vivid portrayals of two strong leaders.

## Back up your points

It is crucial that you refer to the poems in detail throughout your essay. The examiner will, of course, know all the poems well — but you will still need to use quotations to prove the points you are making. A good way to remember this is to PEE on your work: make a <u>P</u>oint, provide the <u>E</u>vidence (a quotation) and <u>E</u>xplain why the quotation is relevant. The quotations should be brief and pithy. Here's an example from an essay: the point is in blue, the evidence is in orange and the explanation is in green.

> **The Duke is a harsh man, used to being in control.** He chooses 'Never to stoop', which suggests he enjoys being dominant over others, particularly those he sees as of a lower status. **Ulysses, however, treats his sailors more humanely.** He refers to them as 'Souls that have toiled, and wrought, and thought with me', which implies that he sees them as his equals and respects them.

Don't just list features in a poem. You'll get no marks for pointing out a simile, but you'll get lots if you explain *how* it contributes to the poem.

## Spelling and punctuation

A maximum of three marks will be given for accuracy — so it really is worth reading your work through carefully when you have finished writing to check that it makes sense. It could make the difference between a good grade and a great grade.

# Practice questions

Higher-tier and foundation-tier questions are very similar. The key difference is that foundation-tier questions include more guidance and tips; higher-tier candidates have to brainstorm the hints for themselves.

Have a go at these sample questions. Plan your answers as if you were about to tackle each question in the examination.

## Higher tier

1 (a) **Compare how the poets present emotions in 'The Song of the Old Mother' by W. B. Yeats and 'The Laboratory' by Robert Browning.**

(b) **Now go on to examine how emotions are presented in two poems from the list below:**
   **'Havisham' (Duffy)**
   **'Salome' (Duffy)**
   **'Stealing' (Duffy)**
   **'Kid' (Armitage)**
   **'Those bastards in their mansions' (Armitage)**
   **'Hitcher' (Armitage)**

2 **Death is a theme shared by many poems in your *Anthology*.**

(a) **Choose either 'Education for Leisure' or 'Anne Hathaway' by Carol Ann Duffy and compare the poet's attitude to death and how death is presented with either 'November' or 'I've made out a will' by Simon Armitage.**

(b) **Consider 'The Eagle' by Tennyson and one other poem from the Pre-1914 Poetry Bank about death; compare and contrast the poets' attitudes to death and how they present this theme.**

3 **'By using a persona, a poet can reveal the heart of another human being.'**

(a) **Choose one poem by Carol Ann Duffy and one poem by Simon Armitage that you could use either to support or to contradict this statement.**

(b) Choose two poems from the Pre-1914 Poetry Bank, one of which could be used to support the statement and one of which could be used as evidence against it. Explain your choices through close reference to both poems.

4 (a) Compare the ways in which Carol Ann Duffy presents relationships between people in 'Elvis's Twin Sister' and one other of her poems.

(b) Choose two poems from the Pre-1914 Poetry Bank that also each feature human relationships. What do you find similar and different in the ways that these relationships are portrayed?

## Foundation tier

1 (a) Compare how the poets present emotions in 'The Song of the Old Mother' by W. B. Yeats and 'The Laboratory' by Robert Browning. Remember to compare:
  * the feelings in the poems
  * how the poets show the feelings through their writing

(b) Now go on to examine how emotions are presented in two poems from the list below:

'Havisham' (Duffy)

'Salome' (Duffy)

'Stealing' (Duffy)

'Kid' (Armitage)

'Those bastards in their mansions' (Armitage)

'Hitcher' (Armitage)

Again, remember to compare:
  * the feelings in the poems
  * how the poets show the feelings through their writing

2 Death is a theme shared by many poems in your *Anthology*.

(a) Choose either 'Education for Leisure' or 'Anne Hathaway' by Carol Ann Duffy and compare the poet's attitude to death and how death is presented with either 'November' or 'I've made out a will' by Simon Armitage.
  * How does each poet present death?
  * What do they feel about the deaths they describe?

(b) Consider 'The Eagle' by Tennyson and one other poem from the Pre-1914 Poetry Bank about death. Compare the ways in which each poet presents death and how they feel about the deaths they describe.

3 'By using a persona, a poet can reveal the heart of another human being.'

(a) Choose one poem by Carol Ann Duffy and one poem by Simon

Armitage that you could use either to support or to contradict this statement.

(b) Choose two poems from the Pre-1914 Poetry Bank, one of which could be used to support the statement and one of which could be used as evidence against it. In each case, explain your choices through close reference to both poems. Remember to comment on:
* the language and imagery used by the poets
* their attitude towards the characters that they are presenting

4 (a) Compare the ways in which Carol Ann Duffy presents relationships between people in 'Elvis's Twin Sister' and one other of her poems.

(b) Choose two poems from the Pre-1914 Poetry Bank that also each feature human relationships. These can be parent/child relationships, or the relationship between lovers (or a husband and wife), or between masters and servants.
* What do you find similar in the ways that these relationships are portrayed?
* What do you find different?

# What does it take to get an A grade?

The criteria that the examiners use to mark your essays are carefully designed to help you get the best mark of which you are capable. Examiners mark what you have written and not what you *haven't* written (or, in other words, you won't lose marks if you miss out a couple of points). So it's up to you to write about the poems in as much significant detail as possible. You can see from the grade guidelines below what it takes to earn a top mark.

**Grade A** Candidates respond critically and sensitively to the poems, taking into account alternative approaches and interpretations. They explore and evaluate the ways meanings, ideas and feelings are conveyed through language, structure and form, making connections and comparisons between them.

**Grade C** In responding to poems, candidates show understanding of how meanings and ideas are conveyed through language, structure and form. They explore connections and comparisons between the poems, referring to details to support their views.

**Grade F** In giving personal responses to poems, candidates show understanding of key features, including themes and language. They make straightforward connections between the poems, and refer to aspects of texts when explaining their views.

# Sample answer

Here is a sample answer to higher-tier question 1. It would earn an A* grade.

**1 (a) Compare how the poets present emotions in 'The Song of the Old Mother' by W. B. Yeats and 'The Laboratory' by Robert Browning.**

Introduction: defines the emotions the essay will cover

There is bitterness apparent in both these poems from the Pre-1914 Poetry Bank. The Old Mother is resentful of the 'young [who] lie long and dream in their bed' while she has to do all the work, despite her age and approaching death. The anonymous narrator of Browning's monologue is vengeful towards her lover and his new partner — so much so that she is planning to kill her rival with poison and apparently takes much pleasure in doing so.

Viewpoint and audience

Comparison

Example of:
**point**
evidence
explanation

Both poems are written in the first person and, in both cases, the male poet has taken on a female persona. It is not clear, however, to whom either poem is addressed. The Old Mother is perhaps talking to herself — it could be that the poem, with its mixture of iambic and anapaestic beats, helps her to get through the day, like the work songs of sailors or slaves: 'I <u>rise</u> in the <u>dawn,</u> and I <u>kneel</u> and <u>blow</u>'. 'The Laboratory' is also written in the present tense. While many of the girl's words are clearly directed to the alchemist she is employing ('Which is the poison to poison her, prithee?'), **other more introspective phrases suggest that the wronged lover is constantly thinking about what her lover and rival are doing at that moment and how** 'only last night, as they whispered, I brought/My own eyes to bear on her'. It is as if she is rationalising to herself the reasons for having to take revenge.

Focuses on features of language

Example of:
**point**
evidence
explanation

The wronged lover shows her emotions in a number of ways. She is clearly impatient to see her rival dead: she encourages the alchemist by using alliterative phrases ('moisten and mash up thy paste,/Pound at thy powder') and by urging him to work speedily: 'Quick — is it finished?', 'Is it done?' She has been hurt and wishes to see her rival feel pain too: 'Not that I bid you spare her the pain'. **However, she questions the alchemist relentlessly** ('That in the mortar — you call it a gum? ... is that poison too?'), indicating that she has not been so carried away by her jealous and vengeful emotions that she cannot take a genuine interest in the processes that she is witnessing.

Contrast:
tone, mood

The emotions felt by the Old Mother are shown to be less passionate. She is a tired, aged woman who longs for rest. There

is the feeling that she has not got the energy to use any adjectives to describe her day — it is as much as she can do to articulate in simple verbs that she 'must scrub and bake and sweep'. Her bitterness towards the young rich people (presumably her young employers) comes across in the simple comparisons she provides between her own busy day and their lethargy and vanity: 'And their day goes over in idleness,/And they sigh if the wind but lift a tress'.

Conclusion of this section: personal response

Perhaps the ending of each poem best shows the contrasting ways in which the women deal with the emotion of bitterness. The final emotion we see in 'The Laboratory' is excitement as the wronged lover rushes off to administer the fatal dose: 'next moment I dance at the King's!' However, the Old Mother is becoming worn down and she knows it. The fire metaphor in the final line suggests that the very life within her is 'feeble and cold', and there is nothing she can do. We sympathise with her.

**(b) Now go on to examine how emotions are presented in two poems from the list below:**
**'Havisham' (Duffy)**
**'Salome' (Duffy)**
**'Stealing' (Duffy)**
**'Kid' (Armitage)**
**'Those bastards in their mansions' (Armitage)**
**'Hitcher' (Armitage)**

Introduction and theme

I have chosen to write about 'Salome' and 'Kid' because these poems present feelings of bitterness and show how individuals deal with that emotion.

Viewpoint and audience

As with the pre-1914 poems, both are written in the first person and from the point of view of a persona (although here a female poet writes about a woman and a male poet writes about a man). It is not clear to whom Duffy's Salome is talking, but it seems to be someone she knows well. Her tone is casual yet intimate: 'I'd done it before...woke up with a head on the pillow beside me'. Robin in Armitage's 'Kid' is apparently addressing Batman, but we wonder whether he is really talking to his former father figure or whether the words are what he would say if he ever met him again. He is very confident, calling Batman 'big shot' in a disparaging way and claiming to enjoy images of Batman hungry, with 'next to nothing in the walk-in larder', and bored.

Comparison

Example of:
point
evidence
explanation

Tone

Example of:
**point**
evidence
explanation

Focuses on features
of language

Salome does not seem like someone who is used to feeling deep emotions. She admits that she 'needed to clean up [her] act' and 'cut out' her promiscuous lifestyle. It is clear that she has never loved any of the men she slept with: she can't remember any of their names and has a careless attitude: 'what did it matter?' She describes John using the clichéd (yet ultimately ironic) simile 'like a lamb to the slaughter': she seems to enjoy making conquests. Even when she finds a man's severed head in her bed she does not seem shocked or terrified. It is not clear from her comment 'and ain't life a bitch' whether she feels more sympathy towards herself or John the Baptist. She is bitter that it happened, but otherwise almost emotionless.

Contrast:
tone, mood

In contrast, Robin, celebrating his new-found independence, is full of excitement and exhilaration. He's proud of himself and lists the changes in him to prove it: 'I'm taller, harder, stronger, older.' His constant use of slang shows his new assurance, and his bitterness towards how Batman used to treat him is shown by his exagger-ated exclamations: 'Holy robin-redbreast-nest-egg-shocker!' He has no regrets: 'I turned the corner', 'now I'm the real boy wonder.' His emotions are shown through his attitude: he is sufficiently sure of himself to make jokes, even to mimic the Batman theme tune through the '-er -er -er -er' rhyme scheme.

Conclusion: refers
back to the question;
personal response

The four poems deal with feelings of bitterness from four different people in four very different situations. The emotions of each are illustrated through the words and tone adopted by each persona. I was struck by the apparent lack of emotion of Salome, the exuberance of Robin the Boy Wonder, the eager vengefulness of the wronged lover and the sad acceptance of the Old Mother.

# Answers

Answers to 'Review your learning' questions.

## Context (page 8)

1 Armitage
2 Duffy
3 Duffy
4 Armitage

## Themes (page 72)

1 Duffy themes: women, memory, parents and children, love, outsiders
2 Armitage themes: family relationships, attitudes to death, gaining independence, love
3 nature
4 war
5 Some examples are given below.

|  | Duffy | Armitage |
|---|---|---|
| **Family; parents and children** | 'Before You Were Mine' | 'Mother, any distance greater' |
| **Love** | 'Havisham' | 'Homecoming' |
| **Death** | 'Salome' | 'November' |
| **Conflict** | 'We Remember Your Childhood Well' | 'Those bastards in their mansions' |

## Style (page 82)

1 False
2 True
3 True
4 False — this is an example of rhyme.
5 False — it is written in trochaic pentameters.

For the longer questions, you might have included ideas like these:

6 Duffy's poem 'Salome' includes rhyme. The irregular '-ter' rhyme adds humour and pace. It gets more intense near the climax of the poem and the final punchline ends with the rhyming word 'platter'.

7 'I've made out a will' by Armitage includes some striking enjambement; the opening three lines provide an effective example. The first line sets out to surprise us, as there is a pause between 'myself' (so we wonder what he is going to do) and his statement that he is leaving himself to the National Health Service. 'Use' at the end of the second line rhymes with 'glues' in line 3. It seems a very ordinary type of word to describe something so important, and thus provides dark humour.

8 Both 'Stealing' by Duffy and 'Hitcher' by Armitage include the use of the vernacular. Both characters portrayed are outsiders. The fact that they do not use formal English emphasises this, as well as making the characters themselves more believable.

# Glossary of literary terms

**alliteration** The repetition of the first letter or sound of nearby words to create an effect. The strong alliteration in this example suggests the power of the eagle: 'He clasps the crag with crooked hands' ('The Eagle', Tennyson).

**ambiguous** This describes a word or phrase that has more than one meaning, or could be read in two ways. The description of the Duchess's death in 'My Last Duchess' is ambiguous: 'I gave commands;/Then all smiles stopped together.' We are not exactly certain *how* the 'smiles stopped', but we feel sure the Duke killed her.

**archaic** Describes words or phrases that are no longer in everyday use.

**assonance** The repetition of a vowel sound (or a similar vowel sound) in nearby words to create an effect. In this example the assonance on the long vowels 'o' and 'a' suggests the lengthy wait: 'The long day wanes: the slow moon climbs' ('Ulysses', Tennyson).

**autobiographical** Relating to the author's own life.

**blank verse** Lines of unrhymed iambic pentameter verse, as in Browning's 'My Last Duchess'. It is a traditional style in English literature; Shakespeare's plays are in blank verse.

**caesura** A break mid-way through a line of poetry, often to give a sense of balance, as in 'Tichborne's Elegy':

My tale was heard,/and yet it was not told,
My fruit is fallen,/and yet my leaves are green.

**consonance** The repetition of consonants within nearby words to create an effect. In this example, consonance combines with alliteration to show the rush of the water: 'His r̲ollr̲ock highr̲oad r̲oar̲ing down' ('Inversnaid', Hopkins).

**dramatic monologue** A long poem in which one speaker addresses an imaginary audience, such as Tennyson's 'Ulysses'.

**elegy** A poem of mourning for the dead, such as Jonson's 'On my first Sonne'.

**end-stopped** Finishing with a full stop or other punctuation to mark a pause at the end of a line of poetry. This example is from Goldsmith's 'The Village Schoolmaster':
> There, in his noisy mansion, skilled to rule,
> The village master taught his little school.

**enjambement** Lines of poetry that are not end-stopped, but where the sense flows into the following line, are said to be enjambed. This device can be used to make blank verse sound natural, and to create other effects. Hopkins uses it in 'Inversnaid' to suggest the constant flow of water: '…the fleece of his foam/Flutes and…'

**euphemism** A phrase that attempts to avoid embarrassment or unpleasantness. For example, 'passed over' is a euphemism for 'died'.

**first person** Written from the writer's point of view. 'I' is used: 'I think my love as rare' ('Sonnet 130', Shakespeare).

**hyperbole** A deliberate overstatement to create an effect. Armitage says his new house has 'acres of walls' and 'prairies of…floors' ('Mother, any distance greater') to suggest that the task of decorating appears to him almost impossibly huge.

**iambic** Consisting of iambs — metrical feet made up of one unstressed syllable followed by one stressed, such as 'I do̲'. Five iambs in a row make an **iambic pentameter**. This is a perfect example: 'To stri̲ve, to se̲ek, to fi̲nd and no̲t to yi̲eld' ('Ulysses', Tennyson).

**irony** Occurs in an expression that has two meanings — an obvious one, and an 'inner', possibly sarcastic, meaning for those in the know. Goldsmith used irony in 'The Village Schoolmaster': 'Twas certain he could write, and cipher too'. On the surface he is praising the skills of the schoolmaster, but we realise it is only faint praise — of course a schoolmaster should be able to write and do arithmetic!

**metaphor** An image that suggests that one thing is something else as a way of comparing them. Clare describes 'clouds sailing to the north' as if they were ships ('Sonnet'), to help us imagine them scudding through the sky. **Extended metaphor** A metaphor that continues over a number of lines or even the whole poem, such as the image of Armitage's mother being linked to him by means of a tape measure ('Mother, any distance greater').

**onomatopoeia** A word that sounds like the item it refers to, like 'buzz' and 'whoosh'. Duffy uses a form of onomatopeia in 'Havisham': 'Whole days/in bed cawing Noooooo at the wall' and 'Don't think it's only the heart that b-b-b-breaks'.

**oxymoron** A contradictory phrase that sounds impossible on first hearing but which actually contains some truth, such as 'inhuman men' ('The Affliction of Margaret', Wordsworth).

**pentameter** A line consisting of five metrical feet; see also **iambic, trochaic**.

**persona** A role taken on by a writer. The writer pretends to be someone else and writes from that person's viewpoint. Examples include Wordsworth in 'The Affliction of Margaret' and Browning in 'The Laboratory'.

**personification** Talking about an object or an animal as if it were a human to create an effect, as in: 'Till stars are beginning to blink and peep' ('The Song of the Old Mother', Yeats).

**pronouns** Words like *it*, *its*, *they* used to avoid repeating the name of an object or objects. **Personal pronouns** are words like *I*, *you*, *he*, *she* used to avoid repeating the name of a person or people.

**pun** A play on words, such as 'bloody queer' in Armitage's 'My father thought it bloody queer.' The poet plays with the idea that 'queer' can mean both strange and homosexual.

**quatrain** A stanza of poetry that is four lines long. Browning's 'The Laboratory' is made up of 12 quatrains.

**refrain** A line (or lines) that recurs at the end of stanzas in a poem, such as 'And now I live, and now my life is done' in 'Tichborne's Elegy'.

**rhetorical question** A question that is asked for effect, without an answer really being expected: 'What would the world be, once bereft/Of wet and of wildness?' ('Inversnaid', Hopkins).

**rhyme** The repetition of the same sound at the end of nearby lines of poetry, such as 'wet'/'met' and 'face'/'place' in 'The Man He Killed' by Thomas Hardy. **Half-rhyme** is near rhyme, such as 'shackles'/'ankles' in Armitage's 'Those bastards in their mansions' and 'glitter/'platter' in Duffy's 'Salome'. **Rhyming couplets** are pairs of iambic rhyming lines, such as the conclusion to Shakespeare's 'Sonnet 130': 'And yet, by heaven, I think my love as rare/As any she belied with false compare.' **Heroic couplets** are long series of rhyming couplets, often used in dramatic monologues, so called because they were used by ancient Greek poets when writing heroic tales of battle.

**second person** Written as if directed at a particular person. 'You' is used, as in Armitage's 'Homecoming': 'midnight when you slip the latch'.

**simile** An image that compares one thing to another using 'like' or 'as'. In 'like a thunderbolt he falls' ('The Eagle', Tennyson), we appreciate the sudden speed and immense strength of the bird.

**symbol** A thing, usually a physical object, representing or suggesting something non-physical; for example, a tape measure to represent the mother–son bond ('Mother, any distance greater', Armitage).

**syntax** The grammatical construction of a sentence.

**tenses** **Past tense** is used for what has already happened: 'she smiled, no doubt, /Whene'er I passed her'. **Present tense** refers to what is happening now: 'I call/That piece a wonder'. **Future tense** describes what will happen: 'we'll go/Together down, sir.' (All these examples are taken from Browning's 'My Last Duchess'.)

**theme** An idea or subject explored by the poet; for example, grief.

**third person** From an observer's or an outsider's point of view. 'He' or 'she' is used: 'He kissed the child, and by the hand led,/And to his mother brought' ('The Little Boy Found', Blake).

**trochaic** Consisting of trochees — metrical feet made up of one stressed syllable followed by one unstressed, as in the line 'Batman, big shot, when you gave the order' ('Kid', Armitage).

**vernacular** Everyday language as used by ordinary people, especially slang.

**word play** Usually refers to double meanings (puns).